Questions You Shouldn't Ask About Christianity

Though this book is designed for group study, it is also
intended for your personal enjoyment and spiritual
growth. A leader's guide is available from your local
bookstore or from your publisher.

Copyright 1987
Beacon Hill Press of Kansas City
Kansas City, Missouri

Printed in the United States of America

ISBN: 083-411-1225

Contents

Chapter 1 **Is the Bible Really True?**   4
            T. Crichton Mitchell

Chapter 2 **Why Are There So Many Bible
            Translations?**   14
            Leslie R. Keylock

Chapter 3 **How Was Life Created?**   28
            Max Reams

Chapter 4 **What's Wrong with Doubting God?**   36
            Deborah Detering

Chapter 5 **Why Is the Old Testament God
            So Cruel?**   41
            Mark Davis

Chapter 6 **Why Does God Allow Suffering?**   47
            Kenneth E. Schemmer

Chapter 7 **Why Doesn't God Answer Prayer?**   59
            Lloyd John Ogilvie

Chapter 8 **Isn't the Devil Just a Myth?**   69
            Charles R. Gailey

Chapter 9 **Why Do Christians Join Cults?**   76
            Harold Bussell

Chapter 10 **Why Are There So Many Hypocrites
            in the Church?**   87
            Stephen M. Miller

Chapter 11 **How Do We Know Jesus Was
            Resurrected?**   96
            Rod Huron

Chapter 12 **Isn't Hell Just a Scare Tactic?**   108
            D. James Kennedy

Chapter 13 **How Do I Know There's a Heaven?**   117
            D. James Kennedy

Chapter 1

Is the Bible Really True?

by T. Crichton Mitchell

Background Scripture: Isaiah 44:24—45:7; Ezekiel 26:1-14

THERE ARE at least a half dozen reasons why I believe the Bible is true. They range from the accuracy of its history to its influence on people today. And they include the witness of archaeology, the fulfillment of biblical prophecies, the authentication of recorded miracles, and the marvel of the Bible's own survival.

The Jews Preserved It

One reason I believe in the accuracy of the Bible is because of the meticulous and painstaking care with which "the Chosen people" of the Bible preserved, transcribed, and guarded the Old Testament. Now remember, the Old Testament is far from complimentary to the Jewish people: in many places it exposes them as an ungrateful nation, rebellious against the one true God who "visited and redeemed" them out of Egypt, made a nation of them, and gave them a privileged and strategic place among the nations of the East. It is these very histories that record Israel's dreadful failures. And it is in these preserved stories that the nation's greatest kings are besmeared and blotted with wrongdoing.

It is amazing to me that a nation should endure defeat in battle, oppression, exile, holocaust, and near extinction, and through it all struggle at the expense of terrible sacrifice to preserve the records that condemn them. Is it at all reasonable to suppose that the Jews endured all this, just to bequeath to posterity a bundle of forged, inaccurate scrolls?

At the modern end of the story, since 1948 the State of Israel has found that the Old Testament is the textbook of national recovery, a guidebook to the constructing of a new land. Three thousand years ago the founding generations were given, and discovered, many agricultural and industrial secrets that really worked. After three millennia, their children are putting them to work again and making their little land the envy of the surrounding nations.

The Israeli settlers of the early fifties were inexperienced in farming, and the land was largely an unknown quantity; but the Old Testament came to their help. Dr. Walter Clay Lawdermilk, expert in agricultural science, wrote:

> Fortunately the Bible tells us what plants can grow in particular places. We know, for example, from the book of Judges that the Philistines grew corn . . . olive groves . . . vineyards—all these plants are doing well there today.[1]

In the southlands of the Negev the rainfall is less than six inches a year. What can grow in that? But the new settlers remembered the stories of wells dug there by Abraham and Isaac (Genesis 26:17-18). They searched, surveyed, and eventually found the old wells still there, choked with the sands of the centuries but still holding Isaac's "springing water" at their depths. Not the bitter underground water of the surrounding Negev, but pure, clear drinking water. Today settlements grow and prosper there, and scores of families build houses where their ancestors had pitched tents. Hagar's well alone, mentioned in Genesis 21:14-19, supplies close to 100 families.

Modern Israelis plant trees where Abraham planted them; in fact, they planted 2 million tamarisks where he planted one (Genesis 21:33). The mountains once so naked are now clothed with trees and greenery. One Jewish professor I know says, "We are relying on the Book of books!" This nation has learned in less than 40 years what it has taken other nations centuries to discover.

Archaeology Supports It

History and archaeology are Siamese twins. For the last century and a half the vast earth-mounds of the Middle East, called "tells" by the natives and scholars, have been coaxed to reveal their secrets to the archaeologists who have unearthed vital facts from the graves of former civilizations.

Already, enough has been uncovered to make a firm case for the truth of the Bible on archaeological grounds. As Bible scholar Joachim Rehork says:

> Is the Bible always right? We shall certainly be able to answer in the affirmative for those passages which have been confirmed by non-biblical parallel sources or by archaeological discoveries. The Bible can claim another form of "rightness," however, insofar as it brings nearer to us its times and the people of its times with their ways of thought and behaviour so that we learn how better to understand their sermons, parables, allegories, visions, symbols, and allusions. Perhaps we shall some day be in a position to affirm, even of passages which are still unclear and puzzling to us today, that the Bible is right after all, as seen through the eyes of the people of its times![2]

The tells in the Middle East are telltales from which "the stones (and other things) cry out." They are layer cakes of long-vanished cultures, nature's history book in earthly Braille. Vast libraries of the "finds" and their interpretation are housed in cities across the world, especially in Jerusalem, Cairo, London, and New York.

In the years between 1923 and 1929 the hometown of Abraham at Ur of the Chaldees was methodically uncovered. Five colossal temples were exposed, one of them 100 yards by 60 yards, with walls thick as a fortress and with the kitchens of the priests—still in working shape. Ur was no small city. Abraham's hometown had been noble, cultured, and idolatrous. From this noble city and its gods, the Lord called Abraham to become the father of all who believe. By 1929 the spades had sliced through layer after layer, with each layer telling its own earthly tale.

But the most thrilling discovery of all at Ur was that of an eight-foot water-laid strata of clean clay and sand. On top of it were signs of civilization, and under it there were also signs of occupation. This revealed a radical interruption of life and culture. Archaeologist Sir Charles Leonard Woolley charted four distinct levels in this tell; he numbered them from the surface downward. Under the surface, at level one, were the graves of ancient kings. Level two yielded pottery and domestic utensils. Level three was the layer of clay 8 to 10 feet deep. And level four revealed many vessels and tools that date back to before the time of the great Flood. Woolley wrote: "We have found the Flood." About 16 feet below a brick pavement that could be dated at about 2700 B.C., they found the ruins of Ur which had existed before the Flood.

Werner Keller sums it up:

> Other archaeologists discovered a further important checkpoint near Kish, southeast of Babylon, where the Euphrates and the Tigris flow in a great bend towards each other. There they found a similar band of clay, but only 18 inches thick. Gradually by a variety of tests the limits of the Flood waters could be established. According to Woolley the disaster engulfed an area northwest of the Persian Gulf amounting to 400 miles long and 100 miles wide, looking at the map we should call it today "a local occurrence"—for the inhabitants of the river plains it was however in those days their whole world.
>
> After endless enquiry and attempts at some explanation, without achieving any concrete results, any hope of solving the great riddle of the Flood had long since been given up. It seemed to lie in a dark and distant region of time which we could never hope to penetrate. Now Woolley and his associates had through their tireless and patient efforts made a discovery which shattered even the experts: a vast catastrophic inundation, resembling the Biblical Flood which had regularly been described by skeptics as

either a fairy tale or a legend, had not only taken place but was moreover an event within the compass of history.[3]

It would probably be unwise to say that Woolley's "flood" was, without a doubt, the biblical flood; but traces of the same flood have indeed been discovered elsewhere in Mesopotamia—Kish, Fara, Nineveh, for example—and were recorded in Flood stories on tablets found with about 2,000 others at Nineveh and now in the British Museum in London. These are called "the tablets of Gilgamesh," after a legendary king who tells on the tablets a Flood story almost exactly like that of Noah's.

In our own generation, former astronaut Jim Irwin and his colleagues have searched for the remains of a large ship thought to have been grounded near the summit of a mountain in Turkey, encased in ice, and reportedly seen by at least 10 people at different times—a shepherd, an archdeacon, three Russians, and four American airmen. Perhaps our search for Noah's ark is still unfinished?

Additional archaeological discoveries that help confirm the truth of biblical history included the discovery of Jacob's well at Sychar, the synagogue at Capernaum, and the structures of Herod the Great. Of even more importance were the discoveries at Ras Shamra in Syria in 1929, at Jericho in the 1950s, at Nag-Hammadi in Egypt in 1954, and supremely the Dead Sea Scrolls in the caves of Qumran in 1947. In addition, in 1959 more biblical scrolls were discovered, adding to the accurate materials on Isaiah, the prophets, and fragments of other parts of the Old Testament, notably Exodus 13:1-16 and Psalm 15.

Such discoveries, together with accurate deciphering and translating, encourage us to see in the Bible a true and trustworthy document.

Fulfilled Prophecies Defend It

Let's take the matter from yet another angle. The prophecies in so much of the Bible illustrate in their fulfillment the Scripture's trustworthiness.

The prophets of the Bible often predicted events far in advance—sometimes hundreds and even thousands of years ahead. Frequently later Bible authors record the fulfillment, but often the task is left to secular historians who may even be unaware of the prophecy whose fulfillment they are in fact substantiating. Beyond this, it frequently was the case that the person fulfilling the prophecy didn't know anything about it.

Consider Cyrus the Great, Persian emperor of whom the Lord declared through Isaiah, "I summon you by name . . . though you do not acknowledge me" and who yet carried out to the letter the declared intention of God, some 200 years after Isaiah had prophesied them (Isaiah 44:24—45:7). Witness also the rise and fall of the four great monarchies, exactly as predicted by Daniel in chapters 2 and 7. There's a magnificent confidence in the divine messages that are revealed through the prophets of the Bible. The Lord seldom troubles to prove His ways to men, and the prophets see no reason why He should. But the fulfillment proves the authenticity of the prediction.

The destruction of Jerusalem was predicted by Jeremiah (26:18), by Micah (3:12), and was repeated by Jesus Christ (Mark 13:2). This prophecy was fulfilled through a heathen general entirely unaware of either the prophecy or the prophet; Titus was the unaware Roman who at the fall of the Holy City in A.D. 70 called for a plow and used it to indicate to posterity the leveling of the magnificent towers of the city. And as prophesied, the city became "as a plowed field."

There is also the phenomenon that some of those predictions were delivered far in advance, in direct opposition to current trends, against all reason. And yet later Bible writers or secular historians recorded the event as it happened.

An example of this is in the prophecy by Ezekiel (26: 4-5, 14; 47:10). It seemed absurd. Whoever heard of "nets drying on the sea"? And who in his right mind would predict the utter destruction of Tyre, a flourishing kingdom, so strongly defended and seemingly impregnable that it held up the great Alexander on his way to conquer Egypt? But God, through Ezekiel, said, "I will scrape away her rubble and make her a bare rock." At one time Tyre was on the coast. But to improve its defensive capability, it moved to a nearby island. In order to conquer it, Alexander was forced to build a giant causeway, or earthen bridge, so he could invade Tyre by both land and sea. And he built this causeway from the ruins of the former Tyre. So the old city became "a bare rock." The causeway later became a place where fishermen did dry their nets.

It's a Book Man Could Not Write

The Bible is not so much a book as a library of 66 books, written in 3 languages, by at least 40 authors, from different cultures, with diverse backgrounds and training, over a span of at least 1,600 years. Connivance? Forgery? Or is it the product of the Eternal Spirit of God?

Its teachings on morality and ethics, in total opposition to selfishness and sin, illustrate the truth of philosopher Francis Bacon's words: "The Bible is such a book as man could not write if he would, would not write if he could!"

For Christians the acceptance of the Old Testament by Jesus Christ constitutes one of the strongest of all reasons for accepting and trusting it. The Christian faith stands or falls with the divine character of its founder, Jesus. The New Testament is not alone in presenting Him as the greatest and wisest person who has ever lived: historians, philosophers, theologians, and great minds from all walks of life have agreed that Jesus Christ of the first Christian century was all that God could be expected to be if He became man.

Even the most radically hostile critics hesitate to reduce Jesus Christ to anything less than the greatest teacher of all time. And even on this unsatisfactory premise it should be important that He was so fully convinced of the truth of the Old Testament. And of course, He is the content of the New Testament. In Him are fulfilled scores of prophecies related to every phase of His life (see Luke 24:27, 32; Acts 10:43).

With these things in mind we assert He:

1. Was God who came to earth.
2. Accepted the entire Old Testament as God-given, even the disputed sections that some Bible scholars struggle with today: Deuteronomy, Jonah, Lot's wife, Solomon's glory.
3. Used the Old Testament personally (Matthew 22:29; Luke 4:4; John 5:39).
4. Promised us the New Testament (John 14:26; 16: 13-14).

Many other points come to mind on the subject of the Bible's reliability. But I haven't the space to discuss miracles, errancy vs. inerrancy, and the history of translation and textual problems. Let me say simply about my Bible:

- There is science here, but it is not a book of science.
- There is religion here, but it is not a book of ritual.
- There is classical literature here, but it is not a literary textbook.

The Holy Bible is a book about God, man, and salvation, and its truth is fully demonstrated in its achievement of objective.

The Bible is true. Let its critic tell me:

1. How else could it be so harmonious with universal law?
2. How else could it so precisely predict distant events and persons?
3. How else could it mold the character of society, nations, people?

4. How else could it adhere so closely to its plan to save humanity from sin?
5. How else would it have been so fully trusted by Jesus Christ, the Incarnate Word of God?

It Changes People Today

I conclude with a stronger reason why I believe the Bible is true, namely the proven relevance of the promises of the Bible. Whatever is really true will be universally valid: it will be true in life and experience, true yesterday, today, and tomorrow.

What the Bible teaches about God, Jesus Christ, salvation, deliverance from sins, inward peace, have been verified by an endless line of believers from the very first men and women of God until now.

Ancient and modern, rich and poor, ignorant and learned, old and young: the witness to the truth of the biblical promises is nothing less than an avalanche of personal proof. There would be little possibility of even scratching the surface of this vast mountain of proof of the truth of the Bible promises: hundreds of promises validated by millions of witnesses. Who but a closed-minded person would choose to ignore this?

Solid evidence of the truth of the Bible surrounds us daily, probably hourly, if only we would open our eyes to the miracle of the changed lives we know.

Let us remember that God's word in the Bible, obeyed and trusted, can result only in His blessing. But ignored, flaunted, or disobeyed, it will result in calamity just as it did for the faithless and rebellious Hebrews of Old Testament times.

1. Werner Keller, *The Bible as History* (London: Hodder and Stoughton, 1965), 429.
2. Ibid. (Revised edition, 1980), 438.
3. Ibid., 28.

T. Crichton Mitchell is professor of church history at Nazarene Bible College, Colorado Springs.

Chapter 2

Why Are There So Many Bible Translations?

by Leslie R. Keylock

Background Scripture: Psalm 119:97-106

TWENTY YEARS AGO when he was a young man study-
ing for a doctorate, George Martin was challenged at a weekend retreat to read the Bible. He went to a local bookstore,
thumbed through a number of translations, and chose the
New Testament in Modern English by J. B. Phillips. "It
caught my eye, I bought it, prayed that God would speak to
me through it, and read it," Martin says. Today George Martin is the editor of *God Speaks Today,* one of the largest daily
devotional guides to Bible reading for Catholics.

Far more Bible translations line the bookstore shelves
than when George Martin made his choice. Most of us need
a more thorough guide to Bible translations than might have
been necessary back then. Also, churches and Sunday

Schools need thoughtful recommendations to help them choose a Bible for church use.

When more translations appear, more Bibles are sold. Sales figures confirm this. In addition, different translations meet the needs of different people. A person who has never read the Bible before will not want the same translation as the seasoned Bible student who wants to know what the original Hebrew and Greek have to say.

Of course, the "original Bible" was not a single document but a whole series, written over the centuries by many

different authors. What we have today are copies of copies, some of them very close to the original manuscripts, but none of them from the hand of the original author. And translation is not a simple restatement of individual words from one language to another.

In this century the demand for a more appropriate Bible in contemporary English has so far produced over 75 translations, according to Wayne Walden of Harvard University. In three decades since the publication of the watershed *Revised Standard Version* in 1952, the need for a modern English Bible translation has become so acute that no less than 11 major translations or editions are now available to satisfy almost every type of Bible reader. The names, dates of publication, and common abbreviations are:

King James Version	1611	KJV
Revised Standard Version	1952	RSV
New American Standard Bible	1960	NASB
New English Bible	1961	NEB
Jerusalem Bible	1966	JB
New American Bible	1970	NAB
The Living Bible	1971	TLB
Good News Bible	1976	GNB
New International Version	1978	NIV
New King James Version	1982	NKJV
Reader's Digest Bible	1982	RDB

What are the strengths and weaknesses of each of these? What kind of influence are they likely to have in the immediate future? To provide answers to these questions, some of the nation's leading Bible scholars gave their evaluations.

King James Version

Nearly everyone has recognized the literary beauty of the King James Version (KJV). It is still the best-selling version on the market, but it suffers from two major handicaps. First, the English language has changed so much over the years that young people and new Christians have found its sentences as difficult to understand as the English of Shakespeare's plays, which comes from approximately the same time. The average reader has no way of knowing that "I prevented the dawning of the morning" (Psalm 119:147) means "I got up before dawn." Second, so much new information about Bible times has been discovered that the KJV is now often inaccurate. Gerald Hawthorne, professor of Greek at Wheaton College, says, "The KJV will probably be relegated some day to the place of a literary masterpiece that will no longer be read by the average church member."

Even Arthur L. Farstad, chairman of the *New King James Version* translation committee, sees the KJV's diminishing use: "Eventually it will have to become a historic piece like the Geneva and Coverdale Bibles, too archaic for common usage.

Jack Lewis, professor of Bible at the Harding Graduate School of Religion in Memphis, adds a word of caution, however: "The KJV has been buried so many times and it hasn't died, so announcements of its death may be premature!"

Revised Standard Version

The earliest of the newer major translations still being purchased in significant numbers today is the *Revised Standard Version* (RSV). Sponsored by the National Council of Churches and published in 1952, it has recently sagged in sales. Most evangelicals have been somewhat cautious about it because they are not happy with the NCC. But the recent sales slump, according to most observers, is because those who read the Bible have moved on to more modern translations. Ronald Youngblood, professor of Old Testament and Hebrew at Bethel Seminary West in San Diego, says the RSV will "suffer the fate of the KJV, especially among younger people." The irony is that when the RSV first appeared, many Christians criticized it for being too modern!

Whether the revision of the RSV will revive its career or

whether it will hasten its demise remains to be seen. One task of the committee doing this revising is to attempt to eliminate what chairman Bruce Metzger, professor of New Testament language and literature at Princeton Theological Seminary, calls its "overmasculinization." Some conservative Christians have reacted strongly against this change, but evangelical scholars admit that sometimes masculine words have been used in English that do not occur in the Hebrew and Greek originals. For example, Psalm 143:2 says, "No man living is righteous before thee," but "man" does not occur in the original. (The NIV translates this, "No one living . . .") They respect the RSV for its scholarship but conclude that, in the words of Donald Carson, professor of New Testament at Trinity Evangelical Divinity School, "It will have a future in nonconservative circles but not elsewhere."

The Living Bible

The Living Bible (TLB) is not really a translation. It was an attempt by one man to put the Bible into a language his children could understand. Knowing neither Hebrew nor Greek, Kenneth L. Taylor, then editor of Chicago's Moody Press and now president of Tyndale House Publishers, produced a highly popular, readable, contemporary interpretation that has sold well, contrary to anyone's expectations. An example of Taylor's contemporary touch is the description of Job as "the richest cattleman in that entire area" (Job 1:3).

Scholars agree that the TLB has helped convert many non-Bible-reading Christians to Bible reading and has been an ideal first Bible for young people and family devotions.

But like any one-man translation it suffers from the limits of what one person can know, and lacks the checks and balances provided by a committee. (Amos 1:1 consists of a mere 12 words in Hebrew; the TLB has 30.) Donald Carson notes that reading comprehension is no higher for the TLB than for the *New International Version,* and adds that Taylor's doctrinal views are visible in both the translations and the footnotes.

Taylor is continuously revising the TLB, however, and a number of scholars believe it will be influential for many years.

New English Bible

The first British Bible to break completely with the King James tradition was the *New English Bible* (NEB). In an effort to produce a work that was both accurate and literary, the translation committee included both biblical scholars and men of letters.

Scholars have applauded the beauty of its English. Gerald Hawthorne, for example, praises it for "some marvelous phrases," and calls it "a superior translation."

But the NEB has nevertheless not done well in evangelical circles in America. Americans object that it is "too British," but even the English have not welcomed it. Donald Carson objects that it is "so consciously aristocratic" and has "the bias of the Oxbridge intelligentsia." Ronald Youngblood says, "Even people in England can't understand it." As a result, other translations are more popular even in the Church of England. Arthur Farstad says, "I understand whole warehouses are full of them and efforts have been made to force them on churches and factories in England."

More serious is the charge that the NEB translators took undue liberties with the text. Jack Lewis objects to "too much rearranging" of the verses, and Gordon Gee, professor of New Testament at Gordon-Conwell Theological Seminary, protests that it contains "too many exegetical options that are the point of view of a small number of scholars, not proper for a translation." In the NEB, 1 Corinthians 7:36, for instance, is made to refer to celibate marriage, though few scholars support that translation.

A second edition of the NEB is now available, after a revision process of several years. The NEB has not caught on well. Whether the revisions will be radical enough to make it more acceptable remains to be seen.

Good News Bible

The *Good News Bible* (GNB, also called *Today's English Version*) has sold well. Translated by Southern Baptist Robert Bratcher and sponsored by the American Bible Society, it is the first "dynamic equivalence" translation; that is, Bratcher and the committee of scholars who assisted him did not try to make a literal translation. Instead they asked, "What does the biblical text mean?" Then they tried to find the equivalent meaning in contemporary English. For example, the fourth beatitude reads, "Happy are those whose greatest desire is to do what God requires; God will satisfy them fully" (Matthew 5:6).

The GNB has been widely used by the American Bible Society as a pattern for vernacular translations on the mission field. Kenneth Barker says, "The GNB is an outstanding example of the principles of dynamic equivalence." Gerald Hawthorne adds that "the GNB is highly accurate," though many evangelicals question the characteristic use of "death of Christ" in the place of "blood of Christ." The principles of dynamic equivalency were developed by evangelicals such as Eugene A. Nida and Kenneth L. Pike of the Wycliffe Bible Translators. Wycliffe stresses accuracy, not word-for-word translation.

How influential will the GNB be in the United States? Jack Lewis feels it has its place as a Bible with a simplified vocabulary and contemporary language, so it will continue to circulate widely.

Critics of the GNB note, however, that it has its faults. *Newsweek* said it is "useful for new readers, but short on poetry and majesty." Of course, anyone who objects to the philosophy of dynamic equivalency will find the GNB "too free."

Metzger points out, however, that "the GNB is the best

translation for non-church people because of its read-ability," though he admits "it is not a study Bible for church members."

New American Standard Bible

Kenneth Barker divides modern translations into three types: literal, mediating, and free.

The most literal, word-for-word translation on the market today, everyone agrees, is the *New American Standard Bible* (NASB). A surprise best-seller among studious Bible readers, it has sold very well, despite what many feel is its atrocious English—in Gordon Fee's words, "English as it was never spoken by anyone!" For instance, Ephesians 1:4-5 reads, "In love He predestined us to adoption as sons through Jesus Christ to Himself, according to the kind intention of His will."

Donald Carson respects the scholars behind the NASB and feels the Old Testament is better than the New Testament. "But its literalness makes it a poor translation; its English is choppy and appalling."

The NASB is a conscious attempt to revive the *American Standard Version* of 1901. Unfortunately, that translation never gained a wide audience, and the NASB is likely to follow in its steps. Gerald Hawthorne opposed the idea of trying to revive the ASV from the very beginning and feels now that the NASB is often not as good because it is so wooden and literal. Bruce Metzger sees it as having "a rather limited appeal," but argues, "We need it among the versions —though not in the pulpit."

As Ronald Youngblood comments, however, "The NASB will probably remain the favorite of those looking for an ostensibly word-for-word translation, thinking it is much closer to the intent of the original author."

New King James Version

In August 1982 Thomas Nelson Publishers completed

what *Newsweek* called "the most expensive Bible project in history." A team of 130 scholars worked on the *New King James Version* (NKJV), published at a cost of $4.5 million.

The NKJV stays close to the original KJV but replaces archaic words and phrases with contemporary parallels.

The purpose of the NKJV, as stated in the Preface, is to "maintain that lyrical quality which is so highly regarded in the *Authorized Version*" and preserve its form, precision, and devotional quality.

The updating of the KJV has been consciously conservative. The translators of the NKJV have retained words for ancient objects for which no modern substitutes exist, such as *chariot* and *phylactery*. They have also retained hallowed theological terms such as *propitiation, justification,* and *sanctification.*

But they have replaced *thee, thou, ye, thy,* and *thine* with *You, Your,* and *Yours.* All verbs ending in -eth and -est have been modernized. Subject headings have been put in italics, poetry is written as poetry, and modern punctuation marks have been introduced.

Much scholarly response to the NKJV has raised questions about it. Jack Lewis questioned the market for such a translation. "The die-hard KJV people won't use it, and young people prefer to read the Bible in modern English." (The publishers point out that die-hard KJV people and young people *are* using it.)

Fee and Metzger wonder about the wisdom and accuracy of the title. Metzger also objects to the capitalization of pronouns for deity. "Even the KJV doesn't capitalize such pronouns."

More serious, perhaps, is the charge that the NKJV didn't make enough changes. Donald Carson says, "The NKJV isn't modern enough, and is too awkward and heavy. It may be a halfway house for some KJV readers, but they will move on."

The major objection these experts had to the NKJV was

its dependence on the same outdated manuscripts used by translators of the KJV. Other modern translations are based on manuscripts that are older (from the fourth century) and supposedly more reliable than the ones available to the KJV translators.

However, Arthur Farstad, chairman of the NKJV translation committee, rejects this suggestion. "The KJV translators had more manuscripts than people realize. The best come from the fifth, sixth, and ninth centuries. Just because the [other] manuscripts come from the fourth century, they need not be better."

Farstad is enthusiastic about the future of the NKJV. "Along with the NIV, it has a good chance of being one of the two top Bibles."

Reader's Digest Bible

In September 1982, after two years of planning and four years of production, the *Reader's Digest Bible* (RDB) appeared. It claims to be the first condensation of the Bible. In its short life it has already been the subject of evangelical wrath and cartoon satire. (One such cartoon shows the editor tossing a coin and saying to his staff, "OK, it's settled then. Heads we'll kill 'Thou shalt not steal,' or tails, 'Thou shalt not commit adultery'!")

To be fair, however, the RDB states that it was not intended for the person who is already reading the Bible, but for the person "who has little or no knowledge of the Bible ... the person who reads the Bible ... only selectively ... young readers who have *never* read the Bible." It was designed to supplement, not replace, the complete Bible.

To help such readers, Bruce Metzger and the Bible scholars who worked with him condensed the RSV translation of the Bible from almost a million words to about 600,000.

Evangelical Bible scholars have been basically positive about the RDB. Jack Lewis says, "I don't think the RDB people thought churchmen would go overboard for it. It's not going to take the place of other versions. But modern pagans might move from it to a more detailed Bible. Of course, everybody is unhappy with what is left out. But it should be treated like a children's story Bible."

Donald Carson agrees, with qualifications. "In a sense it would do in a milder way what the TLB did: act as a hook to get people to read the Bible. But my question is why it was necessary with so many readable Bibles already on the market."

Metzger sees the RDB as another way of reaching those who have neglected to read the Bible. "It is a kind of evangelistic tool to arouse some people alienated by the Bible's length and complexity."

The strongest criticism has been to the introductions to some of the books, which adopt critical views of the Bible, which most evangelicals strenuously oppose. Arthur Farstad, for example, says, "Initially I felt the RDB had some merit and would help some people. But the introductions alienated me completely; they are all slanted to liberal views. So now I wouldn't give it to anyone on the planet! It's a dangerous book for the uninformed."

Jerusalem and New American Bibles

Among Catholics the *Jerusalem Bible* (JB) and the *New American Bible* (NAB) have replaced all earlier Bible translations. In the last decade the number of Catholics doing daily Bible study has greatly increased, and George Martin, editor of *God's Word Today,* feels that both the JB and the NAB will have a future in Catholic circles. "They will continue to be used by the growing numbers of Catholics who are starting to do personal Bible reading and study," he says.

Noted Catholic Bible scholar Daniel Harrington mentions that the JB has been criticized for its dependence on the French version and the NAB for its occasional clumsiness and inconsistencies. "The two translations complement each other, the NAB being the one usually read in public worship, the JB almost always smooth and readily understandable. Like the NIV, the NAB stands between the RSV and the GNB, while the JB is more like the NEB."

Protestant reaction has varied from appreciative to ecstatic. Lutheran Bible scholar Frederick W. Danker says the NAB deserves, for the present, the designation *"the* American Bible." Gordon Fee agrees: "Except for some Catholic idiosyncrasies, for me personally, it is *the* Bible, much better than the RSV."

By contrast, Ronald Youngblood reacts similarly to the JB, though it annoys him at times. "The JB is a Bible I become alternately ecstatic and enraged about. Its phraseology is especially happy. But the notes are very opinionated and represent the liberal end of the spectrum." Arthur Farstad also objects to the impact of older liberal Protestant views in the footnotes. "The JB has many fine literary touches, but the footnotes often cancel out what the text is saying."

Both the JB and the NAB are being revised.

New International Version

The translation that appears to be rapidly developing into the closest thing to a standard Bible among evangelical Bible-reading people in America is the *New International Version* (NIV). Almost every scholar consulted gave it enthusiastic applause.

Produced by a team of 115 scholars over a period of seven years at a cost of $2.25 million and published by the Zondervan Publishing House, it has gained the acceptance of a wide spectrum of readers. Its sales have been rapidly escalating since it appeared in 1978 and now rival those of the KJV. In fact, in monthly sales tallies recently, the NIV has unseated the No. 1 KJV several times. Richard Ostling of *Time* says the NIV "may be the Bible that finally breaks the King James hold on evangelical and fundamentalist Bible buyers."

Most significantly, the NIV has been adopted as the Bible for use in church services in many circles. Gordon Fee thinks the NIV "is fast becoming the pew Bible of evangelicals, as the RSV has been for mainline denominations." He places the NIV between the now-conservative RSV and the GNB. "The NIV doesn't go beyond the GNB, but it is in the same ballpark. It is, however, more careful, more sensitive to evangelical shibboleths, and more open to traditional terminology."

The NIV has already been officially approved by a number of evangelical denominations. A number of Sunday School publications are using it. The Navigators have adopted it for use in their Bible memorization programs. Even such mainline denominations as the Episcopal church have liturgical commissions considering its official use. Kenneth Barker predicts that "the NIV will stand the test of time and will be one of the few current translations that will endure. I expect it will eventually enjoy the most widespread use among evangelicals, evangelical churches, and a significant number of nonevangelicals."

Bruce Metzger also sees the NIV as the "standard" Bible of the future among evangelical Christians. He even feels the NIV "has it over the RSV" in contemporary language.

The NIV has also become part of the family devotions of many Christians. "In our family," Donald Carson says, "we use the NIV all the time. I hope my five-year-old will treat it the way I treated the KJV. It has the best chance of capturing the support of the majority of English-speaking evangelicals worldwide over the next 50 years." Gerald Hawthorne says, "The NIV is one of the very best translations in American English today for church services and personal study. It is close to the Hebrew and Greek text without being too literal. My wife, who grew up on the KJV, loves the NIV and says it is like reading the Bible for the first time."

More conservative scholars such as Arthur Farstad also praise the NIV for its accomplishments, but they add reservations. "I agree that the NIV is beautifully done in a good English style. But I have a problem with its precision. Is it close enough to the original? For example, it leaves out connectives in some cases that change what the writer said. In 2 Peter 2:1 it leaves out the Greek connective and turns Peter's long sentence into two crisp sentences. But it's no longer what Peter said. The NIV does that far too often."

Despite some criticism, no other modern translation has begun its journey so auspiciously. It would seem that we will see much more of the NIV in the years to come.

Editor's Note: The 10 best-selling Bible versions, as reported in the August 1987 *Bookstore Journal,* are as follows.

1. King James Version
2. *New International Version*
3. *New King James Version*
4. *The Living Bible*
5. *New American Standard Version*
6. Spanish Bibles
7. *Revised Standard Version*
8. *Today's English Version (Good News Bible)*
9. *The Amplified Bible*
10. Interlinear and Parallel Texts

Chapter 3

How Was Life Created?

by Max W. Reams

Background Scripture: Genesis 1—2

FOR MANY PEOPLE, the universe just exists and there is
no Creator. But Christians look with awe at the universe and
say that God created it all. Though all Christians agree on
the *who* of Creation, they disagree sharply on *how* God created things.

Modern science began several hundred years ago. And
when it did, the first scientific discoveries shocked the religious world. For example, most people—Christians included
—thought Earth was the center of the universe. Galileo's
telescope proved that idea wrong. Early clashes between scientists and theologians made it painfully clear that the Bible and science had to be reconciled. But this was easy to say,
and not so easy to do. Many scientific discoveries didn't fit
the theology of the Middle Ages.

Today, science is still a challenge to many Christians.
Astronomy says we live on a tiny planet moving around a

medium-sized star, nestled in a galaxy with 100 billion other stars. Our galaxy is but one of billions of galaxies in the vast universe. Geology explains that fossils and rocks have taken

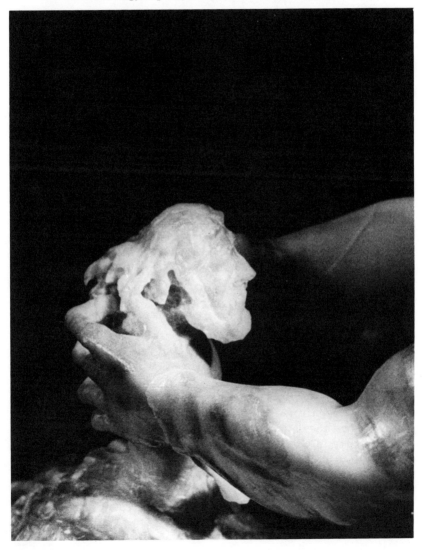

millions of years to form. The Earth is ever active, with the outer layer broken into plates, and shifting about, generating earthquakes, volcanoes, and mountains. Physics describes matter and energy with mathematical equations and traces creation back billions of years. And no respected scientist seems interested in talking about how God fits into the scheme of things.

Biology generates the biggest shock for most Christians. It teaches that all life, including humans, may be related as a result of evolutionary changes that have taken place over the eons. Evolution disturbs some Christians so much that they don't know what to do.

I once prayed with a teenager during a youth camp. He was converted and later returned to be sanctified. I felt he was headed for a life of service to God. Then he entered a state university and enrolled in a biology course. During his studies, he reviewed the evidence for evolution. Someone must have convinced him he had to choose between religion and science. And since he discovered that the evidence for evolution was strong, he gave up his faith. What a tragedy.

Because of stories like this, too many Christians are afraid that science is the enemy of God. Their way of avoiding the conflict is to avoid science. This is the ostrich approach. Christians stick their heads in the sand and hope the problem will go away. I know a Christian science teacher who doubles as an ostrich. He simply will not discuss the theory of evolution. But this kind of approach won't help anyone.

Other Christians prefer an Alexander the Great approach—they attack science. They feel science is wrong, so they try to change it. This approach doesn't work either. Modern science is built on millions of bits of information. So for every shred of evidence we toss out, a thousand new bits of evidence seem waiting to take its place. Revising science is not the Christian's task.

Merging Science with the Bible

Many of the first scientists had a better idea. Most of them were men of faith, who tried to mesh their science with the Bible. They believed that science agreed with the Scriptures, because both were from the hand of God. They worked hard to relate their findings to their faith.

So what happened? Why don't scientists do that today? The early scientists were scholars who talked with other scholars. But before long, science became practical. The Industrial Revolution showed how scientific discoveries could be important in a workaday world. New inventions made life easier. And people began looking to science to solve their problems. Science became like a god to many people. Eventually, society became more secular—and because science was now closely linked with society, most scientists became more secular. And these secular scientists had no interest in relating their findings to the Bible.

Today, secularists present only their versions of new theories. Christian scientists are so few in number that their interpretations of the same theories are rarely heard. Some of the new theories hit hard at commonly held religious views. The Big Bang origin of the universe, the Protoplanet origin of the solar system, the Punctuated Evolution of life, and other theories like these are difficult for many Christians to accept. You see, we Christians have to consider whether or not these theories square with the Bible. Nonbelievers don't have this problem. So they don't even touch on the matter. But for Christians, the problem is very real. We can't ignore the difficulties.

If direct attacks on science are a waste of time, what can we do?

A better approach is to follow the lead of early Christian scientists. They believed that science and Christianity could not conflict. God is the Author of the Bible and Nature, they believed. He can't contradict himself. Today, many Christian scientists try hard to resolve apparent conflicts. These Christians work and witness within the scientific establishment, and they interpret science from a Christian viewpoint.

I wish I could say that all Christians favor this approach, but that isn't so. There is too much disagreement and fighting between Christians. And this weakens the church's witness. Light, not heat, is the believer's responsibility when science and religion seem to be in conflict. Christians need to cooperate with one another in order to influence the scientific thinking of our society.

Evolution versus creation is one of the most talked about science-religion topics today. And for far too many Christians, evolution is dealt with through emotions, not through facts and logic. Christians need to study evolutionary theory to understand the problem.

When Charles Darwin first published *The Origin of Species,* Christians reacted in two ways.

1. Some said evolutionary changes in life can't match the Bible account of Creation.

2. Others said evolutionary changes could be God's way of creating new species.

Darwin's theory was accepted by most biologists. Then, as later discoveries were made, biologists modified the theory.

There are six basic evidences for evolution. These include: differences in fossils from rock layer to rock layer, similarities of body form between groups of animals or plants, changes in or loss of body parts, changes in the heredity of experimental organisms, similarities in the biochemicals found in supposedly related life forms, and similarities between embryos of different animal or plant groups. The meaning of each evidence has been, and is still being debated.

On the creation side of the debate is a group of Christians who call themselves "scientific creationists." But I have to say that most scientists today do not take them seriously; the creationist arguments are seen as weak and unscientific.

These creationists dispute the theory of evolution, and as evidence they cite the claim that no evolution is going on now, or has since Charles Darwin drafted his revolutionary idea. They say we've observed species becoming extinct but no new species being formed. They also ask evolutionists for any laboratory evidence that suggests life can be created from something nonliving. For this, they say, is what proponents of the Big Bang theory contend. This theory says the universe was once a "primordial egg" of great density and undetermined size, and that an explosion scattered the matter and started the universe on its outward expansion.

Creationists also say there was once a global, catastrophic flood. In fact, some cite the existence of fossils as evidence for this. Fossils, they explain, are created when something is quickly buried—before it has a chance to decay or be eaten. (Other creationists explain fossils by saying God put them there to confuse people. But noncreationist Christians respond by indicating they wouldn't want to serve a God who would trick His people.)

For further evidence of a global flood, creationists cite the rapid extinction of dinosaurs, and the fact that three-fourths of the Earth is made up of sedimentary rock—made from sediment.

What Christian Biologists Believe

All scientists debate theories as a way to test them. And evolution is no exception. One of the main concerns of biologists today is how evolution might work. And even Christian biologists disagree on this subject.

1. Some Christian biologists believe that all life was created rapidly. "Scientific creationists" are in this group. They believe that each species was created separately, with no ancestors. No evolution has occurred since creation, except perhaps some microevolution (changes within a spe-

cies, but not enough changes to transform the subject into a new species). Examples would include changes in average height of humans and the fact that in the U.S. we now have many varieties of sparrows—most of which came from the one variety that was introduced into the country. Creationists explain that the potential for these forms of microevolution were written into the genes of humans and sparrows.

2. Others believe that all life was created slowly—even over billions of years. So God's creative acts formed an evolutionary tree of life. All species developed as a result of changes in other species. God's method of creation was evolutionary.

3. One group believes that all life—except human life— was created slowly. God used evolution to create all life except humanity. People were specially created.

4. Still others believe that all the major *groups* of life were created rapidly, followed by slow development into the many different species. For example, the original horse was a rapid creation. Then, the earliest horse population evolved into the many different types of horses we find in the fossil record, as well as those living today. God's creation, according to these theorists, involved limited evolution.

No Christian believes in an atheistic form of evolution. The Bible forbids giving credit for creation to anyone or anything but God. The only evolution permitted by the Bible would have to be directed by God.

Christians disagree strongly on how much God-controlled evolution might have occurred. Some believe only in an instantaneous creation from nothing. Opponents argue that God used already existing matter (dust) to make man (Genesis 2:7). They point to the time gap between the making of man's body and the creation of his soul. These Christians believe that the evolutionary creation of the human body took billions of years. The soul was provided later to make man. Other Christians argue that the creation account in Genesis is not intended to describe specific, scientific events. They say that the purpose of Genesis is to show that God made everything. Genesis doesn't tell us how God did it.

With so many Christian views, can anything be settled about evolution?

How Christians Should Approach the Issue

The first thing Christians should do is listen to each other. We must stop fighting over *how* God made the world. The Gospel is hindered when Christians argue too much. We can have different opinions, but we must accept each other. The secular world watches Christians fight over many small issues. How can we win them if we bicker and fuss at each other? Jesus said, Christians are supposed to show unity (John 17:20-22). John tells us to love one another (1 John 4:7). Some Christians deeply involved with the creation-evolution controversy say that anyone who disagrees with their particular interpretation of Genesis isn't a Christian. Such attitudes hurt the church.

Non-christians distract Christians with evolution. A student once used this ploy to get me sidetracked. I wasted my witness by defending a particular view of creation. We never got around to discussing how all of creation is a powerful evidence of a living God.

Creation is a beautiful concept. It can be used to lead people to the Lord, but we must be careful to avoid side issues. We can declare the basic truths of creation, but we should not force everyone to accept our view of *how* God did His work. Atheistic evolution, however, which leaves out the Creator, is unacceptable.

We probably won't know how God made the world until we reach heaven. But we can know, today, the redeeming love of our Creator God. Let's avoid excessive arguments about God's method of creation and spend our time and resources in witnessing for Christ.

Max W. Reams is professor of geology, Olivet Nazarene University, Kankakee, Ill.

Chapter 4

What's Wrong with Doubting God?

by Deborah Detering

Background Scripture: Genesis 18:1-15; 21:1-7

DEAR ELIZABETH,

Now that you are away from us, your dad and I keep thinking of things we should have talked to you about while you were home. We think you have absorbed some of these things by growing up with us, but we can't be sure. Right now we are wondering if we have taught you how to doubt. The secular, sophisticated world in which you now live will have an effect on your faith; in fact, we would be surprised if you didn't have doubts about Christian doctrine and your relationship to God. So there are some things we want to say to help you deal with doubt in a healthy way.

The first thing to do about doubt is to admit it—to yourself, to God, and, if possible, to other Christians. Just as you can't solve an equation without setting it up properly, you cannot find the answer for a doubt you have not acknowledged. If the Virgin Birth has become a stumbling

block to you, admit it. If you are not even sure of God's existence, tell Him so. It is a contradiction, of course, to talk to someone you don't believe in, but by doing this you refuse to deny God and allow Him to answer you.

If you can discuss your doubts with a good Christian friend or counselor, do so. Don't share your questions with anyone who condemns you for doubting. That kind of judgmental attitude is immature and will only frustrate and confuse you more. Our Lord often answers us through one of His people, but sometimes finding supportive friends is more important than having our questions answered.

Do not fear that doubt will end your relationship with Jesus. Doubt does not have to be the end of commitment; it certainly is not the end of God. His existence is not dependent on your belief; neither is His love for you dependent on what you feel. He helped Dad find work when both Dad and I were discouraged about it. He did not insist that we feel optimistic first. Doubt is only what we think or feel, but commitment is what we will. You can pray, "Lord, I can't see You, I can't feel You, I'm not even sure I believe in You any more, but I will still base my actions on the premise that You are not only out there but right here, and I *will* follow You." Remember that He sometimes draws us closer to himself by seeming to withdraw for a while so we can learn to trust Him more deeply.

Remind yourself of the things you do not doubt. You can say, "I don't understand how You, God, could become human, but I see the stars and know something of Your creative power." Or "I don't know what purpose You have for my life, but I do know that Your love called me to commit myself to You in baptism." Build your confidence with positive statements.

Be patient. If you do not expect to know everything about the chemistry of the body, how can you expect to know much about God? If you spend 12 years learning to be a doctor, shouldn't you spend even longer learning to be the person your Heavenly Father wants you to be? Look at His long-term creative work: His building of mountains and carving of rivers; His Word from Genesis to Revelation; His plan for your development from infancy to adulthood. He will be patient with you as long as you are seeking Him. He demands that you obey, not that you understand everything He does and is.

Learn from other people's experiences with doubt. And don't make the mistake of assuming that real saints live without doubt. Moses doubted that God could use him to speak to Pharaoh; David wondered whether God had forgotten him; John the Baptist had to ask Jesus if He was the Messiah; Thomas wanted proof of the Resurrection; in his own life, John Bunyan met the Giant of Despair; Corrie ten Boom relied on Betsie's faith in the concentration camp.

Your dad and I have also doubted. In the past few months you watched us put our house up for sale, knowing our Lord wanted us to move. But sometimes we panicked because we did not know where He was leading us. We have discussed Christian doctrine with you enough so you know belief has not always come easily to us; by that we have learned to live with doubts even while we live for our Lord. You can do the same.

Let doubt be the beginning of growth and not the end of it. Some young adults decide, "I have grown up and I know that the religion of my youth is a fairy tale. Because I no longer believe, I am mature." You know better. We have not fed you any fairy tales. Some of your friends will lose their faith because they toss out grains of truth along with the mythological baggage. It is tragic when the Resurrection is confused with Easter baskets. Any learning is a process of replacing imperfect knowledge with more correct and complete understanding, and growth in faith is no different.

For example if you find, when you study atomic physics, that what you have believed about atoms was incorrect, you won't (you'd better not) just drop out and claim that atoms aren't real. Instead you will study the text and talk with your professor until your misconceptions are cleared up. Discovering that God does not answer all prayer with immediately satisfying miracles should not lead you to stop praying, but instead to discover how He wants you to respond to Him, and what prayers He wants you to offer.

Growth comes not by saying, "Lord, I quit," but by asking, "Lord, what's next?"

Maintain a regular routine of prayer, Bible study, and fellowship. If you don't, you won't hear God because you are not listening. Just as a doctor reads medical journals to grow in medical knowledge, a Christian needs regular Bible reading to grow in his faith.

Meet with other Christians in informal fellowship and

regular church attendance. Don't, however, confuse good habits with rigidity. You can refresh your faith by changing your patterns of Bible reading, prayer, worship, and fellowship. Try reading and pondering one verse instead of an entire chapter; find an open chapel for private prayer away from your room; explore different fellowship groups to find one that meets your current need, whether a social group, an intimate prayer group, or an intellectual Bible study.

Check your physical condition. Satan makes use of the physical and mental exhaustion caused by a rigorous schedule and the barrage of new ideas to breed doubt and despair. If you are losing sleep, drinking too much coffee, fretting over difficult assignments, or fighting off a sore throat, then doubt will be more a condition of body than of mind. You need to take care of the physical problem first. Remember that Jesus became tired and discouraged, too. Exhaustion is not sin, it is simply part of being human.

We let you go into the world knowing that there will be doubts, expecting that Jesus will lead you through them and hoping that we have taught you how to doubt so you will not be overwhelmed. Remember that what you don't know or can't be sure about is not so important as following Jesus, believing that He does have the answers.

You are precious to us both as the daughter God gave us to rear for Him, and as a sister who follows Jesus along with us. As long as we travel together in His care, you are not far from us.

Love,
Mom

Chapter 5

Why Is the Old Testament God So Cruel?

by Mark Davis

Background Scripture: Deuteronomy 7:1-11

You MUST DESTROY them totally. Make no treaty with them, and show them no mercy."

That's the order Moses gave the children of Israel concerning how to deal with the people in the Promised Land (see Deuteronomy 7:2).

Later, when Joshua led his army into Jericho, he followed those orders. "They utterly destroyed everything in the city, both man and woman, young and old, and ox and sheep and donkey" (Joshua 6:21, NASB).

God's orders to Samuel regarding the Amalekites were much the same. "Now go, attack the Amalekites and totally destroy everything that belongs to them. Do not spare them; put to death men and women, children and infants, cattle and sheep, camels and donkeys" (1 Samuel 15:3).

These are just a few ancient scenes that seem to paint a picture of an Old Testament God who doesn't begin to resemble the New Testament Jesus. God orders the slaughter of women and children. Jesus extends forgiveness to the outcast woman, and He holds little children on His lap.

How are we to reconcile these two images?

This apparent contradiction has led many to conclude that the God of the Old Testament and the Jesus of the New are radically different in both their dispositions and their desires for humanity. The Old Testament God is seen as cruel and vindictive, while the New Testament Jesus is kind and forgiving.

But such a Jekyll and Hyde view of God ignores some of the most fundamental texts of the Bible. Nothing was more basic to the Old Testament believer than Deuteronomy 6:4, "Hear, O Israel! The Lord is our God, the Lord is one!" (NASB). He is one in His nature and one in His purpose for humanity.

It is their one God who has been fully revealed in Jesus Christ. Paul states unequivocally that "in Him all the fulness of Deity dwells in bodily form" (Colossians 2:9, NASB). That means that any contradiction we imagine between God and Jesus is the result of either misunderstanding or unbelief. Seen correctly, God is as He shows himself to be in Jesus. And any thoughts we have about God that cannot be harmonized with His revelation in Jesus are incorrect.

Nothing is more apparent in Jesus than that God loves all people. He extends His love freely and without discrimination to the least and greatest of the world. Because He loves, He wants good for all and harm for none. And the very best that could come to anyone is that they be restored to the image of God—that they be holy.

So because of His great love, God's first concern for all His creatures is their moral health. His great anger with evil grows out of His great compassion for us. He knows what evil will do to those He loves. So in order to preserve the objects of His affection, He must destroy all that would destroy them. Every wrathful judgment in history has been a compassionate act of preservation. God's wrath shows His utter intolerance of all that degrades and destroys. He hates sin as a mother hates the sickness that threatens the life of her child.

The Bible then, both Old and New Testaments, is the record of God's efforts to rescue humanity from the consequences and power of sin, and to bring us back to himself. Every scriptural passage dealing with the severity of God must be examined against the backdrop of His divine passion for human redemption.

Reconciliation between God and humanity can happen only when two things take place. First, people must be made aware of the gravity of sin and the danger ahead if they persist on their present course. Second, God must open a way by which people can be forgiven, reconciled, and made holy. Without an awareness of sin, we will not repent. And without a divine provision, we cannot repent. Both the awareness and the provision require the sternest of measures.

Take, for instance, the conquest of Canaan. This slice of history demonstrates how seriously God takes sin, while at the same time it reveals how God opens the way of salvation to those who will obey Him.

The invasion of Canaan opened a way of salvation because it provided a home for the Hebrews. Within this nation and this geography the drama of redemption unfolded so that salvation became available to the entire world. It was through this very people and in this very land that the Messiah came, lived, died, and rose again—all for the redemption of the world.

But the invasion also revealed God's anger with sin, because the conquest of Canaan served as God's judgment on the people who were occupying the land. Moses makes this clear in Deuteronomy 9:5. "It is not for your righteousness or for the uprightness of your heart that you are going to possess their land, but it is because of the wickedness of these nations" (NASB).

It is a well-documented fact in Scriptures, as well as in secular history, that the Canaanite society and religion was one of the most decadent of that time. For example, it featured human sacrifice—even child sacrifice—to a gallery of gods, as well as the practice of cult prostitution. Israel, then, became God's agent of judgment upon the Canaanites.

Another instance that shows the seriousness of sin, along with God's determination to save, is the later defeat and exile of Israel. Even God's chosen people had to face the consequences of their sin. Not even they were allowed to inhibit the flow of God's grace to the world.

Israel had become wicked—so wicked, in fact, that in some instances she even exceeded the wickedness of her heathen neighbors. So God passed judgment on His own people. As He had done with the Canaanites, He used foreign nations as the agent of His punishment. And the land was devastated by war.

This was not just raw retribution on God's part. His judgment came with an eye toward Israel's seared conscience, and toward those who would be willing to walk through the door of salvation He was providing.

God is determined to save those who are willing to be saved. To accomplish this He will turn the very powers of evil on their head. He'll use the wickedness of the wicked to turn history toward himself. He'll use one evil nation to destroy another evil nation, so that all nations will know how much He wants to bring all people to himself.

God is consistent and unchanging. He's always rich in mercy and He's always ready to save, but He'll save none against their will. If we refuse to say to Him, "Not my will but Thine be done," He will say it to us. At the same time, He'll let no evil group of persons jeopardize the salvation of those who wish to be His.

God's grace is as much in His acts of judgment as it is in His acts of kindness. There's judgment in the New Testament as well as in the Old. And there's grace in the Old Testament as well as in the New. His kindness and severity, both of which are essential aspects of His love, are everywhere apparent.

The Old Testament pattern is one of God giving countless opportunities for the rebellious to repent. In each case, it was only when their refusal was final that the hand of judgment fell.

It was in the Old Testament that He gave the Amorites 100 years to repent, but they would not. Before the Flood destroyed the world, Noah preached for 120 years to his neighbors. And from nations that refused to accept God's grace, He received faithful individuals like Ruth and Rahab the prostitute—both of whom are in the family tree of King David and Jesus.

If grace is seen in the Old Testament, so is judgment seen in the New. Some of the strongest statements of judgment ever made were spoken by Jesus in the "Seven Woes" of Matthew 23; and for the same reason that judgment was pronounced in the Old Testament. God is determined to show sin for what it is.

Yet, in spite of all this, it must be stated frankly that questions remain. Should boys who mock a prophet be killed by bears? Must innocent children suffer the same fate as their wicked parents?

These and other hard questions represent a twin danger to all who would believe. The first danger surfaces when we let such questions detract us from the overwhelming scriptural evidence that God does love all people and has dedicated himself to providing the best for each one of them.

The second danger is seen when those who turn their backs on these hard questions either ignore them or resort to simplistic answers. This is only a more subtle form of unbelief, because it refuses to examine the evidence. Their restless desire to nail down every loose end forces such people to settle for a view of the Lord that is inconsistent with either God the Father or the Son.

What we must do is rest our confidence on that which can most obviously be known about God, and then give Him as long as necessary to enlighten our dim understanding. We should enjoy the abundant assurances in both Testaments that He does love us. And then we should let the seeming contradictions spur us on to a more consecrated pursuit of understanding the God who is revealed in Jesus Christ.

Mark Davis is pastor of the Bauer Wesleyan Church, Hudsonville, Mich.

Chapter 6

Why Does God Allow Suffering?

by Kenneth E. Schemmer

Background Scripture: John 16:20-22; James 1:2-5

> Barbara Clausen and her husband, Paul, served as asso-
> ciate ministers for a number of years before pastoring
> their first congregation. Paul was an especially good
> singer and choir director. Since Paul's devastating ill-
> ness, Barbara has worked full-time as a secretary and as
> a mother in order to raise their two children, now in
> college. She has donated hundreds of hours and dollars
> to help educate people about Huntington's disease. Bar-
> bara tells their story.

YOU WILL SPEND the next 15 to 20 years in slow deterioration and end up in a hospital bed with none of your nor-
mal bodily functions. If you are more fortunate, you will die
of a heart attack or pneumonia at an early age."

Those words were spoken by doctors at the Mayo Clinic
to Paul Clausen, my husband. It's not easy to be given such
a prognosis at 35 years of age.

Paul had been examined and tested for two days, and

his family history reviewed. Then the doctors confirmed the diagnosis of Huntington's disease. "Go home and live with it," they said. "We have no control drug, no cure."

That afternoon and evening we spent the most difficult hours of our lives in a motel room in Rochester, Minn. Another cruel blow hit us as we pondered the future—we would eventually have to tell our two children the facts about the disease and the 50-50 chance that they would inherit it.

Paul enjoyed life. He loved to sing, preach, and be with young people. How would he handle such devastating news? At first he tried to accept the verdict—the "sentence," as he called it—for a crime he did not commit.

Early Symptoms

Our story goes back about 11 years. We did not need a tragedy to bring our family to the Lord. We had served Him to the best of our abilities for many years. We were pastoring our first congregation after many years of associate pastoral work. We enjoyed our two small children, loved our work, and felt very secure. Yet stealthily and cunningly, strange

symptoms began to occur in my husband—fear, fatigue, depression, change in personality, loss of interest in work and in our family. Those symptoms appeared and disappeared in ominous cycles for about 18 months.

During that time we visited local doctors. The diagnoses varied: Paul needed vitamin B-1 shots; was just overtired; was under too much stress; must learn to relax; was in the wrong kind of work. We visited more clinics and hospitals, and finally Paul resigned from our church. We moved to another city for a different environment, and he took a part-time job. The symptoms increased. At last we decided that a trip to the Mayo Clinic would provide a thorough checkup and conclusion. My husband knew of a history of Huntington's disease in his family, since his mother had died of it. But he disliked talking about it—a common characteristic of those having the disease.

Huntington's disease is one of 2,000 known genetic diseases, a neurological dysfunction like Parkinson's disease, multiple sclerosis, and epilepsy. Usually the patient's family history tells the story; the children have a 50-50 chance of inheriting the disease. Identified by Dr. George Huntington over a hundred years ago, the disease began as a genetic mutation and was brought to this country from England in the early 1600s. Until 1967, the few facts and statistics available to the medical profession had permitted only 1,000 positive diagnoses of the disease. Since the organization in 1967 of the Committee to Combat Huntington's Disease, 100,000 cases have been identified. This extremely severe disease causes a progressive mental and physical deterioration for 15 to 20 years and eventually results in complete loss of bodily functions. One by one the good things of life are taken away. It is a hard and cruel death.

Depression and anxiety severely blighted Paul. I watched him go through stages of denial, anger, bargaining. Necessity demanded, finally, that he enter a psychiatric hospital. We both knew then the end had begun. The bottom had dropped out of life.

Despite thousands of prayers for his healing being offered, healing didn't happen. We believed and prayed for a miracle. We attended church services where many pastors anointed and prayed for Paul while the whole church joined in praying for his healing. Letters and cards came from across the country, from around the world, giving us courage. We prayed and waited. It seemed that God had deserted us when we needed Him most. Had He?

I remember walking into our son's bedroom one afternoon to look at the picture of Jesus hanging on the wall. Jesus' arms were outstretched. Through tears I told Him that things were falling apart. He had let us down completely. I couldn't believe that He loved us or cared for us at all. In utter despair I started to leave the room when I seemed to hear the words, *"Where are you going?"*

I stopped and sat on the bed, thoughts flooding my mind. Where *would* I go? What would I do? Our lives had been centered around the church. I looked up at that picture again, and those outstretched arms seemed to be outstretched for *me.* I decided at that moment to trust Him. I knew that my life with its problems would be better with God than without Him.

That decision proved right. God has sustained me and my family more than I believed possible. We've had many problems that seemed to overwhelm us. Most of the time it has required sheer willpower and determination to hang on.

Problems Multiply

I wish I could tell you that after my experience of recommitment things began to go easier and we were able to cope with life a little better. Actually, our problems began to multiply. I had become the family breadwinner, but my salary was inadequate for the many household bills, medical and hospital bills, and unexpected expenses that always seemed to arise.

The events of the next two years seem unreal now, but they happened. Even though we had a major tragedy in our family, we weren't shielded from other problems. It was as if Satan had decided to launch a full-fledged attack designed to destroy not only my husband but me too.

When we moved from our mobile home into a house, we lost money on the sale, just when we needed appliances and furniture. Not long after people from the church came and painted the rooms for us, we noticed soot and dusty cobwebs hanging on the pictures and draperies and walls. The fire chief finally came and found a faulty chimney; everything had to be cleaned, washed, or discarded.

When my sister tried to surprise us at Christmastime by putting decorations on our tree, she laid the tree lights out on the living room carpet to test them; every light burned a black hole in the carpet. When men from the church put up paneling in the bathroom, they laid it out in the kitchen to put glue on the back: the pilot light on the gas stove caused the flammable glue to explode, destroying a chair, curtains, part of the floor, and the cupboards.

The furnace failed in the middle of winter, and we had to get a new motor. In late spring a blizzard blew the television antenna away, along with part of the roof. During a terrible wind and rain storm, I went off the highway at the proper exit but ended up in a viaduct full of water that flooded the car. My son and I had to scramble out quickly.

The following summer our daughter Karen contracted mononucleosis. Shortly after her illness, she and I both had to undergo extensive tests for allergies. Those were just a few of the crises our family faced.

Through all our struggles my deepest and most sincere prayers centered on Paul. I prayed that he would be able to accept his illness and live with it, and that our children and I might be able to love him, care for him, and help him face his altered life. After one particularly bad weekend at the hospital, I drove home feeling discouraged and defeated. I didn't sleep well that night. Frequently I prayed something like this: "Oh, God, let me be able to help him. He has no one else. Let me be able to help him."

A couple of days later I drove to the hospital again, not expecting much of a reception. To my amazement Paul came smiling to greet me. His face appeared relaxed and almost radiant. I knew that something wonderful had happened. Although he had difficulty putting his experience into words, he shared as much of it as he could: He had been sitting alone on a bench in the hospital yard feeling rejected, bitter, and hostile toward everyone. He felt someone sit down at the other end of the bench and looked to see who it was. No one was there, yet he felt a warm presence that moved toward him until it seemed to envelop him completely.

"I felt God again," Paul told me. "I know He's going to be with me. I know He loves me because of you."

I reported the change in him to the doctors. They told me he would slip back into the stages of depression and that many of his former problems would arise from time to time. But let me tell you, their prediction never came true. The children and I enjoy a relationship with Paul that never ceases to amaze us. I must emphasize that the nature of the disease usually causes family tensions and conflicts that are almost never resolved. Many marriages end in divorce or shattered relationships. Our family teetered on the edge of that precipice before Paul had his encounter with God.

Eventually, we transferred Paul to a general hospital only 12 miles from home. We saw him several times a week and brought him home for visits. Everything went well for about eight months, until we found that our major medical insurance was being terminated. Since our medical bills amounted to $700 a month, I could not afford his care without insurance.

After exhausting all avenues of help offered to me except divorce—which would make Paul a dependent of the state—I decided that he should return to the state hospital. Although the decision was very difficult for me, Paul accepted it with great poise and the assurance that everything would work out all right. He now lives in the chronic medical section of the Kalamazoo State Hospital.

Trusting

I cannot assure any individual of divine healing. Dedicated Christians suffer and die every day. Accidents destroy or maim some. Others remain crippled or blind. Christians are not exempt. The old cliché that illness or grief comes into our lives as a test or punishment is dangerous, because it makes a Christian feel as if he has done something wrong when healing does not come. Instead of repeating old clichés, I would rather talk about God's love and grace and the blessings we can continue to enjoy. As Eugenia Price said in her book *No Pat Answers,* what you don't need when your heart is breaking or your mind is shrinking with fear is a challenge to greater spirituality. What you need then is hope; hope that after some time has passed, by God's grace and love you can begin to function again. We need to hear Jesus' statement again and again, "I will be with you always."

Now let me get into what I call the nitty-gritty of the matter. It's not enough for someone just to say "I'll pray for you." Sometimes I need a handclasp that says "I care." Other times I need to be included in what others are doing. The changeover from one style of living to another brought about by separation from a loved one, whether by death or not, is indescribably difficult. I need understanding and patience, because the easiest thing to do in the midst of my grief is to retreat from those around me. What I don't need are the pat answers that are usually thrown my way: "This is God's will for you. God is teaching you a lesson. You'll just have to pray more. You'll have to have more faith."

Perhaps someone can tell me why an elderly man lives on in a nursing home and cannot die, when a young man wants to live and cannot get well. Or why a young girl is killed in a car accident and a Christian woman in her 90s wants to go to be with the Lord and cannot. Or why a longed-for baby is born dead or deformed. Or why a young mother or father is dying of cancer while her or his children need to be parented.

I don't know why millions of people are starving to death while our garbage cans overflow. Does God love them less? I don't know why a family is murdered while sleeping in their home, or why a young boy lies in a hospital like a vegetable as the result of a highway accident.

Paul and I have seen people in all those situations during the years of our ministry. We have watched good people, wonderful families suffer. Many of our friends have died from accidents, cancer, heart attacks, and other diseases. Two of our close friends were murdered.

Homes are wrecked by divorce, children are abused by the thousands, young people are destroyed by drugs, and adults by alcohol. Every week at the Kalamazoo State Hospital I see the worst that life can deal. Those things happen in Christian homes, too. I don't understand it. It's part of a mystery that we can't understand.

But I know this. God loves all of His creation. He loves with a redemptive and everlasting love. I am certain of this: In the midst of tragedy or crisis I must find peace with God or I will perish. I am compelled to decide if God is a punishing, death-dealing God or if He has the same nature as our Lord Jesus Christ, who walked the earth healing, ministering, and, yes, even weeping.

In his book *O Susan,* James Angel wrote about his young daughter's death at age 20 in a car accident. "God comes to us in our crumbling moments. Not with theological rationale but with quiet affection. His promise is power and endurance to those who believe in and wait upon him."

There is only one place where I can find rest for the anxieties of my heart. That place is in the childlike trust that God eventually gives us. If I can firmly believe in the love of God, I can make it.

Another person has said, "God is faith that comes when there is no reason for faith." Clearly, I had to determine my own image of God. I chose to see Him as a caring Jesus. I refuse to believe that Christ loves my family less than He loves yours or anyone else's because physical healing did not come to us.

Helps to Wholeness

Just as there are many hindrances to wholeness, there are also many helps. A modern, understandable translation of the Bible added dimension to my devotions. Good books that deal with the realities of life have been a tremendous source of help. They deal with situations I myself face.

I practice looking for sources of strength in nature, such as seeing a tulip bulb in the fall and imagining what it will look like in the spring. I believe in the Resurrection. As I think of the roots of trees that delve deep into the earth for strength and water, I remember God's strength. Underneath me remain His everlasting arms. I don't get nearly so tired when I remember that God sustains me.

The practice of stewardship has become more important. I give God His fair share of my earnings, time, and service. Attending the worship services of my church fills my empty emotional life. Music in particular provides a great therapy.

My major problems center in loneliness and self-pity. Self-pity caused me to retreat from life, to find comfort only in solitude. Such a course of action proved unhealthy and unwise. Because I had always been a giver, I had to learn how to receive gratefully. I had to put forth the effort to live for my own and my children's sake, rather than for my husband's. Our children Karen, and Dave, express concern and compassion for their dad in their weekly trips to see him. They look for ways to show their love for him. I have been so thankful for their help and encouragement.

In my desperation to seek Paul's healing, I bought books, read articles, and watched televised mass-healing services. I was tempted to take him to such a service. But after much contemplation and soul-searching, I realized that Jesus' first concern is with individuals. He never prayed over a large crowd and hoped that some of them would be healed. Rather, He healed *each* person who came to Him. My heart goes out to the thousands of persons who return home from healing services thinking that God loves them less than He loves others because they are still ill. Some studies have shown that many of those people leave the meeting worse off than before because of the physical letdown and mental depression that follow exposure to such services. Many refuse to take any more medication and die needlessly when doctors and good medication could have sustained them in useful living.

Contemporary Christianity often emphasizes external, spectacular occurrences. I believe the church's real ministry focuses on redeeming souls and teaching people how to cope with the situations in which they find themselves. The Christian's life is not without problems, in spite of what some people say. The lives of Jesus, the apostles, and other Bible personalities were all filled with challenges and hardships. The words of Albert Schweitzer help me: "And to those who obey him, whether they be wise or simple, he will reveal himself in the toils, the conflict, the suffering which they shall pass through in his fellowship. And as an ineffable mystery they shall learn in their own experience who he is."

James Angel's book says, "Faith at its deepest level is trust, hope is confidence, and love is redemptive." I believe that with all my heart. What can separate us from the love of God? Can tragedy? Disease? Can anything really separate us from the love of God unless we allow it to? I believe God works *through our circumstances* as we live within His will. I cannot believe in Him or love Him or serve Him otherwise.

Discussing the apostle Paul, one person said it had been God's will that Paul be in jail so that he could write his great letters to the various churches. Another disagreed. "No, it was God's will that Paul write the letters, but it was the Roman ruler's will that he be in jail."

I like the second person's point of view. Jesus said that while we live in the world we will have tribulation, but that He has overcome the world (see John 16:33). Therefore, we have two possible responses to our suffering: We can become bitter, cynical, and of no use to ourselves or anyone else; or we can accept our circumstances and allow God to work through us and within us.

Recently I reread a Scripture passage that has often bothered me. Many times I've heard people say that we must give thanks *for* everything. I've never been able to be thankful for my husband's illness. I've never been thankful that my children have been deprived of their father and that we had so few years of life and work together.

But as I read that verse again I realized that it says *"In* every thing give thanks" (1 Thessalonians 5:18, KJV, italics added). That's quite different, isn't it? *Within* our circumstances we have found many reasons to be thankful. Strength comes when I think I cannot go another step. Help comes through encounters with people I have never known and in strange places: an elevator, a K-mart garage, a hospital room. Burdens seem lighter when someone walks with me day by day and shares the yoke I bear. I know that redemptive love develops the trust and hope that carry me through each day.

I wish my husband might have been able to share this story with you and express those experiences of his that I will never know. I deeply admire Paul for his courage, trust, and ability to live through this debilitating illness, especially since both of his sisters have died of Huntington's disease during his illness.

When Paul could still talk we often prayed together, sang together, and talked about heaven. He assured me that he will sing again one day, and that he will occupy first chair in the baritone section of the heavenly choir—that is, if he doesn't get to direct the choir! I told him that many of our musically talented friends would be bidding for that job, but they're going to have terrible competition if he really wants it. I know Paul is at peace with God. He has no fear of death, and for that I am grateful.

A beautiful song came to our attention a few years ago. We did not get to sing it together, but we learned to love the words and it became our theme song. This song has been a continual source of strength to me.

He giveth more grace when the burdens grow greater;
He sendeth more strength when the labors increase.
To added affliction He addeth His mercy;
To multiplied trials, His multiplied peace.

When we have exhausted our store of endurance,
When our strength has failed ere the day is half done,
When we reach the end of our hoarded resources,
Our Father's full giving is only begun.

His love has no limit; His grace has no measure;
His pow'r has no boundary known unto men.
For out of His infinite riches in Jesus,
*He giveth, and giveth, and giveth again!**

Chapter 7

Why Doesn't God Answer Prayer?

by Lloyd John Ogilvie

Background Scripture: John 15:1-8; 2 Corinthians 12:7-10

THE OTHER DAY I saw a fascinating sign in the window of one of those speedy printing establishments that promises to reproduce anything while you wait. The sign said, "Quick printing service for those who want everything yesterday!"

I was impelled by curiosity to go inside to ask the owner about the sign. His response was a classic: "We cater to people who put off until the day after tomorrow what they should do today and then when they want something, they want it yesterday!"

That could also be a description of the way many of us deal with the problem of seemingly unanswered prayer. Some of us put off talking to God on a consistent, daily basis. Then a crisis strikes or an important decision must be made. We tell God our need and want an instant response. And we want it yesterday.

But there are also others of us who have experienced what seems to be unanswered prayer, even though we have kept up a consistent prayer life. We, too, become impatient when we have asked God repeatedly about a problem or need and are forced to wait for an answer.

Waiting is not easy for any of us. Impatience is a persistent problem. But waiting for the Lord to answer our prayers is the most difficult of all. We begin to feel rejected, letdown, unloved. We pray for guidance, healing, a resolution of misunderstanding in a relationship, direction for a decision that we must make, the fulfillment of a deep longing. Then the days drag by. No apparent answer seems to come. What is God up to? Doesn't He know how urgently we need His help? And then, to complicate things further, some prayers seem to be answered quickly and others seem to be unheeded by the Almighty.

The apostle Paul, whose life was punctuated by spectacular examples of answered prayer, endured the painful experience of what seemed to be unanswered prayer. In 2 Corinthians 12:7-10, he describes the perplexing dilemma he endured when he prayed that a "thorn in the flesh" be removed from his life. He pleaded with the Lord that it might depart. The prayer was not answered in the way Paul proposed. The nature of the "thorn" is not explicitly revealed by Paul. Good thing. We all have some thorn in the flesh, and therefore all who are afflicted in some way can find comfort and courage in what Paul discovered.

The word for *thorn* in Greek is used for a stake, splinter, or thorn. Whatever the imagery, Paul suffered a physical malady that caused excruciating pain. Expositors have variously suggested eye trouble, malaria, epilepsy, insomnia, and migraine headaches. There are good cross-references to support a case for any of these. Paul is not specific. That enables all of us to share in his pain and his discovery. The apostle is as wise in his reservations as he is in his revelations when it comes to personal exposure. All of us can empathize with

what he endured by giving the thorn our own personal iden-
tification.

Our thorn can be whatever is painful or difficult physically, spiritually, or relationally. It is something we've asked
to be healed or removed, yet have been forced to wait with no
apparent answer to our prayers. For some of us it is a bodily
limitation or sickness; for others, a broken relationship; for
still others, some unsatisfied dream for our lives.

Whatever it is, identify it for yourself and keep it in the
forefront of your mind as we reflect on what happened to
Paul. His thorn is a metaphor for anything that causes us
sorrow. An infected splinter may be as painful as a stake
driven through a limb. What troubles us may seem small
and inconsequential to someone else. But to us it is a stake
of limitation. Whatever it is, this much must be said: It is
ours, and why the Lord does not take it away is our personal
dilemma.

Note the progression as the apostle deals with the perplexity of his thorn. First there is the instinctive desire to
pray, asking the Lord to intervene. Then he experiences the
Lord's strength to endure. Finally, there is the peace of abiding, a sublime acquiescence that is in itself a greater answer
to prayer than Paul anticipated.

The thorns of life drive us to prayer. Paul relates, "For
this thing I pleaded with the Lord three times that it might
depart from me." We wonder if "three times" is a Hebraism
for many times. That would be true for most of us. We have
prayed repeatedly about pain or perplexity, wondering if the
Lord has heard. But all too often our prayer seems to be a
one-way monologue. We don't wait long enough in quiet for
it to be a dialogue. It is as if we made a telephone call to place
an order or ask for instructions and then hung up before the
other person had a chance to speak. "Hello, Lord, this is
what I need. Good-bye!"

Not so with Paul. He waited. And listened. What the
Lord said to him has more residual power than the removal

of the thorn. Listen! Have you ever heard the Lord say this to you? "And He said to me, 'My grace is sufficient for you, for my strength is made perfect in weakness.'"

Did Christ answer his prayer or not? Yes and no. No, He did not give Paul what he asked for. Instead, He gave him an infinitely greater gift and assurance. As we look at the promise in its parts we begin to appreciate its full impact for us.

"He said." Who? The living Christ! The purpose of prayer is to persist until we have made a dynamic contact with the Lord of all life. Christ will not quickly answer if in the answer we are not drawn closer to Him.

"He said *to me.*" Prayer is profoundly personal. We come to Christ with our requests; He begins a renovation of our total life. When I go to my internist with one ailment, he usually wants to give me a total checkup. He is concerned about my total health and well-being. He is not quick to give nifty nostrums that merely Band-Aid what might be a deeper problem. Since I often use busyness as an excuse for neglecting regular examinations, he usually responds to my request for a prescription with, "Why don't you come to my office and let me take a good look at you?"

Our Lord is no less thorough when we come to Him asking for a speedy answer to some need. He wants to talk to us about who we are, really, and where we are going with the precious gift of life. No prayer is unanswered if as a result of lingering in His presence we can say, "He said to me . . ."

And what does He say? *"My grace."* Pause to savor that! Grace is His unmerited, unchanging, unqualified love. With that we have everything; without it, whatever else we might receive is empty. We need fresh grace each day. Prayer is a dynamic dialogue in which we spread out our needs and receive healing love and liberating forgiveness. Conversation with the Lord enlarges our hearts until we are able to receive His Spirit.

He alone is sufficient. "My grace *is sufficient for you."* The word *sufficient* means that the supply is in exact proportion to the need—never too much, never too little, never early, never late. Christ knows our deepest needs. There are times He answers our prayers by not granting our requests. But also, a delay in answering our prayers brings us to the realization that our greatest longing is for the Lord himself. Any quick provision that makes us less dependent on consistent fellowship with the Provider is no answer at all!

And now consider the secret that only the school of what seems to be unanswered prayer can teach. *"My strength is made perfect in weakness."* Christ's strength achieves its purpose in our weakness. The purpose of prayer is not just to make the best of things, but to allow the Lord to use them to make the best of us. Trials and problems give us a grand chance to discover the adequacy of Christ's strength in our weakness.

Often, we want Christ's strength to do *our* will. He waits and puts us through the experience of what we think is unanswered prayer until, more than anything else, we want His strength to do His will. He allows our weakness so that our total dependence is on Him and not on our adequacy. Our subtle sin is to decide what's best for ourselves, ask for strength to accomplish it, and then when we've pulled it off, to forget who made it possible. Christ pulls the rug out from under that kind of pride. For a time our prayers seem empty and ineffective. And finally, in confessing our arrogance, we are forced back to His purpose for us and an abundant supply of strength to accomplish it.

That's what happened to Paul. His response to Christ's answer to what he foolishly thought was unanswered prayer is an expression of profound trust. "Therefore, I will boast all the more gladly about my weaknesses, so that Christ's power may rest on me. ... For when I am weak, then I am strong" (verses 9-10).

A creative sense of weakness is not only facing infirmities but also daring impossibilities. I am convinced that we should be constantly out on the edge of attempting things that we could never accomplish without Christ's power. We attempt far too little and venture with far too much caution. Christ did not remove Paul's thorn, but He made him "more than a conqueror" in preaching the gospel, suffering persecution, enduring imprisonment, and withstanding hardship. By withholding an answer about the thorn, Christ hammered out a mighty apostle capable of surviving thorny circumstances. His no to one thing made possible an obedient man who could appropriate His yes.

Paul's prayer was answered! The power of Christ rested upon him in a new way from that time forward. The word for *rest* in the original Greek meant "to fix a tent upon." This is a bold metaphor. The glory of Christ overshadowed Paul. The Lord's promise "to abide in Me and I in you" (John 15:4, NASB) was fulfilled. Paul's prayers, for a time seemingly unanswered, were answered by the best of all responses. Christ "abided" in him and he in Christ. No prayer can be considered an unanswered prayer if it denies what we want in order to give us what we need. And our greatest need is to abide.

Remember the old spelling bees? They were a source of both pride and panic when I was a boy in grade school. I can remember the teacher lining us all up in front of the classroom. She would give each of us a word to spell. If we spelled it correctly, we remained standing; if not, we were sent to our seats. It really motivated me to learn my spelling lessons! My keen sense of competition made me desire never to be the first to be sent to my seat. And it was always my hope to be the last person standing. The teacher usually started with little words and worked up to more difficult, complicated ones.

Strange how we remember events in our childhood. I'll never forget the embarrassment I felt one day in third grade when I missed a little word in one of those spell-downs. You could have fried an egg on my red-hot, burning, and embarrassed face. The word given to me to spell was *prayer.* I sounded it out phonetically in my mind and then spelled it "p-r-e-y-e-r." I did not know then what I know now: that *prayer for many is preying on God,* a kind of attack, a storming of the gates of heaven for what we want, when we want it, and for our comfort or convenience. It makes all the difference whether our communication with God is spelled with an "a" or an "e."

If I were asked to spell prayer today, I would be sent to my seat again. Prayer is spelled "a-b-i-d-e!" No prayer is unanswered if as a result we abide in Christ and Christ in us.

There is a great promise Christ makes us if we abide. At first it seems to contradict what we've said about unanswered prayer. "If you abide in Me, and My words abide in you, ask whatever you wish, and it shall be done for you" (John 15:7, NASB). The point is that abiding gives us clarity about what to ask. Our desires are transformed in keeping with what is best for us at a particular time.

Christ is for us! He will reorder our priorities, give us strength to endure what He chooses not to change, and give us courage to ask for what He desires to change.

Allow me to draw this into sharp focus with some personal convictions I learned from what seemed to be unanswered prayer.

First of all, I am convinced that Christ knows what is best for me. I have been brought back to that assurance repeatedly. There is no peace until I surrender my circumstances knowing that He will grant me only what will be ultimately good for me. There's so much that I can't see and don't know. Unanswered prayer is really an answer. What I ask for may not have been sufficiently perfected through prolonged abiding. Either the time is not right, or what I've asked for may not be maximum in His plans for me.

Second, I have learned a great deal during the waiting periods. Most important of all, I have found that Christ, not just His answers, is sufficient. Waiting prepares me for what He has prepared and guides me to ask wisely. John Baillie said, "If I thought that God were going to grant me all my prayers simply for the asking, without even passing them under His own gracious review, without even bringing to bear upon them His own greater wisdom, I think there would be very few prayers that I would dare to pray."

Third, I am thankful that the Lord has not answered many of my prayers! As I look back over the years, and contemplate what might have happened if some of them had been answered when and the way I wanted, I am alarmed. I agree with Longfellow: "What discord should we bring into the universe if our prayers were all answered! Then we should govern the world and not God."

Fourth, what I thought was unanswered prayer had led me to discover the formula for creative prayer: Ask once and thank the Lord a thousand times that if the prayer is in keeping with His will, it shall be done. I shared that thought with a friend whose prayers for one of his children seemed to go unanswered. When he prayed, fully surrendering the child's future, and released his worried concern with hourly prayers of thanksgiving, eventually the Lord was able to bless the child in ways that exceeded the man's wildest expectations.

And finally, some prayers seem to be unanswered because we ask the Lord to do for us what He's already guided *us* to do for ourselves. Continual asking becomes an evasion of action. Many prayers are unanswered because we have not acted on previously answered prayer. The Lord will not give us new guidance if we have refused to act on what He's told us to do. Often our prayer channel is blocked by disobedience or unwillingness to forgive or become involved in reconciliation. When we pray for people and are not ready to be part of the Lord's answer with costly caring, He waits until we are willing.

An unconfessed sin of the past or an unsurrendered plan for the future will debilitate our capacity to receive. We cannot expect the Lord's yes to today's prayer if we've said no! to yesterday's answer. Augustine prayed a prayer that will always be answered: "O Lord, grant that I may do Thy will as if it were my will; so that Thou mightest do my will as if it were Thy will." The first part of that prayer makes possible the second. When we want the Lord's will, and do it when we know it, we will be less troubled with unanswered prayer. We'll be too busy dealing with the marching orders of answered prayer!

What I've tried to say in a variety of ways in this chapter is that there is no such thing as unanswered prayer. What seems to be a delay is a special gift to those of us who want everything yesterday. It gives us the wonderful opportunity to discover the greatest answer to prayer for today. We learn to abide in Christ. He is the answer to prayer. His strength is sufficient. Anything else He gives when the time is right will deepen our trust and heighten our praise. But anything without Him is nothing at all!

I will never again use the words, "unanswered prayer."

Condensed from "Why Are My Prayers Unanswered?" in *Ask Him Anything*, by Lloyd John Ogilvie, copyright © 1984; used by permission of Word Books, Publisher, Waco, Tex.

Chapter 8

Isn't the Devil Just a Myth?

by Charles R. Gailey

Background Scripture: Matthew 4:1-11

WELL, isn't the devil as fake as the boogie man and the hobgoblin that kids talk about around eerie campfires, or that special effects experts conjure up for the latest horror movies?

- In 1985, the Los Angeles "Night Stalker" left devil worship symbols at the scene of his killings. When captured in September 1985, he had drawn a satanic star on his arm and a witch's star in a circle on his stomach.[1]
- In Monroe, Mich., 40 miles south of Detroit, a 17-year-old high school student was killed on February 2, 1986 ("Witches Sabbath"), as a "satanic sacrifice." The sheriff said he knew of 12 students who were active in satanic rites. The high school principal added that other area high schools have similar problems.[2]

There was a period when many people doubted the existence of demons and the devil. The 1890 edition of the *Encyclopaedia Britannica* compared the New Testament teaching about demons to the belief in a flat earth. But no more. Now:

- *U.S. News and World Report* estimates that there are 600,000 practitioners of the occult in America.[3]
- An American airline has been offering "psychic tours" of Great Britain.
- It is estimated that there are 3 million Satan worshipers in Germany.
- There has recently been a revival of black magic in France.
- A recent ABC news broadcast estimates there are 100,000 followers of witchcraft in Britain. To supply these disciples, there is even a mail-order house for covens of witches.

Even so, why all the fuss?

Those of us who have lived in the developing world, called by some the Third World, know that the magic and occult that is now invading the Western nations is symptomatic of the battle for good and evil.

Actually, this battle is nothing new.

Long before the Protestant Reformation, the rite of exorcism was being practiced in the Christian Church. And in the Old Testament, you remember Saul's problem with witches (1 Samuel 28).

So before "I Dream of Jeannie" or "Bewitched" materialized on North American television screens, Christians realized there was a battle going on in the world between the forces of good and the forces of evil. Now, at last, the rest of the world is discovering what Christians knew all along. No longer is it just Africans and Haitians who stand in court, accused of killing men and women and cutting them up for medicine, but in Miami a 22-year-old girl recently admitted killing an old man by stabbing him 46 times. After the judge handed down a relatively light prison sentence of seven years, the convicted woman smiled and prayed to Satan in the courtroom. Later she told reporters that she had enjoyed killing the old man.

Are Demons *Really* Real?

Timothy, the young student standing in front of me, fell, straight as a board, flat on his face. Strange words began to pour from his contorted face, and his body began to writhe and wrestle in a terrible display of diabolical power. "Demon possession," my African friends said.

Later, I sat with those friends and we talked about what had happened. As a "green" missionary, I had just witnessed demon possession for the first time.

Many people in modern times have tried to explain away demon possession as epilepsy or mental illness. But those of us who have seen both know that they are not the same. Well-known psychiatrist Scott Peck has witnessed two exorcisms. And in his book *People of the Lie,* he says, "I now know that Satan is real."

Jesus, of course, never doubted the reality of Satan or demons. In the New Testament we read of Christ's numerous encounters with people who were possessed by demons (for example, Mark 5, Luke 8). He did not doubt that they were real. Some scholars, of course, say that Jesus was only reflecting the popular beliefs of His day—that these people were not actually demon possessed. But we must remember that Jesus was Truth in the flesh. There was no falsehood and dishonesty with Him. And, after all, He knew more about the supernatural world than any other person who has ever lived. Furthermore, Jesus could not lie. He reacted to demons as He did because He knew that demons were real.

Jesus cast out demons. He still casts out demons.

When my colleagues and I learned that Timothy had been troubled with demon possession for many years, the vice principal of our college in Africa arranged a time when we could all gather and pray for the student. Unitedly, staff and students prayed in that never-to-be forgotten service.

The demons attacked. In a terrible display of power, Timothy nearly bit off his tongue. But God answered the prayer of His people. That day, the demons came out; Timothy was delivered. When I returned to Africa recently I found that Timothy has never been troubled since that day. Today he is a successful pastor of a church.

Why Are We Hearing More About Demons?

So far, we have seen that: (1) Jesus believed in demons, and (2) we can muster factual evidence of demon possession. But the question remains: Why are we hearing so much about this subject in the Western industrialized nations today?

It seems to me that Russian writer Alexander Solzhenitsyn supplied the answer in his address at Harvard University: "When true spirituality declines, the counterfeit will surface." Today, in this rationalistic, materialist, computer-ized age, horoscopes abound among educated people. Re-cently, on a classical music station in Kansas City, two witches discussed *The Positive Book of Magic.* To top it off, the program was sponsored by a group of obstetricians and gynecologists.

Last year, I walked through the toy department of a large Boston store. Here is what they were selling for the children's Christmas presents: Castle Grayskull: Fortress of Mystery; Dr. Doom and his secret shield; The Other World; and Evil Master of Snakes. This fare was for the *kids!*

Is it any wonder that at the same time we are turning away from God, when we seem to lack any moral backbone, we should see a rise in the demonic?

The Battle of the Ages

The world is a battleground of good and evil. There is the way of Satan, demons, and sin. There is the way of God, goodness, and the fullness of the Holy Spirit. This is the conflict of the ages. There is no neutral ground in this di-vided world.

We cannot ignore the battle between good and evil. My niece works as a computer programmer in a high-rise build-ing in the downtown section of a large American city. Re-cently, the woman she works with said, "I dabble in witch-craft, do you?" Later that week, the woman identified one of the managers of the firm as a warlock.

In this rationalistic age, the ignoring of God's laws and the decline of true religion will only result in yielding to demonic forces—even among computer analysts, teachers, and other well-educated people.

Are You Part of the Problem?

You may be saying, "What do you mean? Do you think Satan will tempt me to become a warlock?" Of course not. Satan is too clever for that. He knows that most people who read this book would be horrified and repulsed by that suggestion. No, his tactic is much more likely to be a blurring of the lines between right and wrong—a gradual and almost imperceptible spiritual decline. As writer Scott Peck puts it, "We become evil slowly, over time through a long series of choices."

Temptations to people who are already Christians are most likely to be along these lines:
- the gradual ignoring of continuing moral decline
- gradually doing things on the Sabbath that you wouldn't have done five years ago
- the telling of a little white lie
- the skipping of devotions with God

Only when our guard is down does Satan see that we are ripe for the entrance of his demonic forces.

The Son of God himself had to fight this battle that is common to every person. In his experience of being "very man," he confronted evil. The battle is recounted in Matthew 4:3-11. Jesus resisted the temptation, and afterward, angels came and ministered to Him.

The beautiful thing about this battle of the ages is that we already know what the outcome will be. The demons know what the future is for them. Satan and all his agents will finally be cast into the "lake of fire and brimstone" and they will be "tormented day and night for ever and ever" (Revelation 20:10).

Meantime, the Christian who is filled with God's Spirit has a special advantage in this battle.

The Best Insurance Policy

And now for more good news. A Christian who has been sanctified wholly has the best insurance policy ever issued against being troubled by demon possession.

All of my African associates testify that they have *never* heard of a person who has been filled with the Holy Spirit being affected by demons. If the Holy Spirit fills you, there obviously is no room left for an evil spirit. This does not mean that a Christian will cease being tempted, but it does mean that as long as a person maintains close fellowship with the Lord in the sanctified life, that person will never be troubled by any demons.

Surely this is one of life's best insurance policies, and one that should bring great peace of mind to the Christian.

Yes, there does exist the power of demons and Satan in this world. The battle between good and evil is real. But this battle of the ages has already been described, and if you are walking in the Spirit, you are on the side of victory. For "the one who is in you is greater than the one who is in the world" (1 John 4:4).

1. *People* Magazine, Sept. 15, 1985.
2. *Kansas City Times,* Feb. 20, 1986, p. A-6.
3. *U.S. News and World Report,* Nov. 7, 1983, p. 83.

Charles R. Gailey is professor of missiology at Nazarene Theology Seminary, Kansas City, and a former missionary for the Church of the Nazarene.

Chapter 9

Why Do Christians Join Cults?

by Harold Bussell

Background Scripture: Acts 2:17-36

TERRY WAS A LEADER in the youth group at the first church I served in California. He'd become a Christian a year earlier and had a glowing testimony.

Then Terry became a Mormon. I still remember his defense: "But Mormons don't drink or smoke."

To Terry, those in the camp of this cult showed more consistency in keeping their convictions, deeper group commitment, and more genuine happiness and sincerity. So he concluded, "They must be more Christian."

During my years of ministry, I've been confronted with many evangelicals who have come out of cults or who are attracted to a cult.

Yet in all my conversations with them, the central issue has never been doctrine. That was usually a minor concern. Something else in the evangelical community is making our people vulnerable to cults.

· Every major cult, with the exception of Eastern groups, began in an evangelical church or with a leader from an evangelical background.

Sun Myung Moon, founder of the Unification Church, was raised in a Presbyterian home. Jim Jones, founder of the People's Temple, professed Christ in a Nazarene church and was pastor of an interdenominational charismatic church and a Disciples of Christ church.

Moses David, founder of the Children of God, had a Missionary Alliance background. And Victor Paul Wierwille, founder of The Way, was an evangelical and a Reformed pastor. Many of the older, more established cults, including the Christian Scientists and Jehovah's Witnesses, also had evangelical roots.

Each of these cults and their leaders share several common ingredients:

First, they all began by defining themselves in opposition to their local church, denomination, or the church at large. They had discovered the "ideal church."

Second, the pastor or leader was placed in a position beyond confrontation. With this came a tight discipleship or shepherding approach to instruction.

Third, these groups emphasized group sharing, testimonies, spirituality, devotions, and, in some cases, Bible study.

Fourth, the leader had gained some "new spiritual insight" emphasizing the last days, healing, community, or spirituality.

Fifth, they placed a high value on community and caring. They also eventually developed their own terminology for their spiritual subculture.

It's easy for us to write off these groups and deny our own vulnerability to deception. But the members of the People's Temple never expected to end up at Jonestown, either.

In my conversations with former cult members and those struggling with cultic leanings, I've found five similarities between cults and evangelical churches that can pave the way for Christians to cross over the line into deception.

The Trap of Personal Experience

We evangelicals place a high emphasis on our experience of Christ; so do the cults. We tend to witness to our conversion rather than about Christ—to the results of the gospel rather than the gospel itself.

But our conversion experience is not the gospel. People also undergo dramatic experiences as they are "converted" by an encounter group, a meditation society, or cultic community. They can also speak of a new happiness, emotional security, or sense of belonging.

The gospel is that Jesus Christ entered human history, died, and rose from the dead. And the new birth is not based on feelings, but on our coming into union with the resurrected Christ—not just any Christ, but He who is God and man at once.

Our conversion experiences vary considerably. Paul faced a dramatic conversion, while Timothy grew into the faith. On the day of Pentecost, Peter made sure that conversion and faith were not mixed. He affirmed the people's response as a gift from God (Acts 2:17-21), but he immediately preached the resurrected Christ (2:22-36). This pattern is followed throughout Acts.

Our tendency as evangelicals to overemphasize our personal experience has some of its roots in the church's reactions to rationalism and liberalism. Rather than emphasizing the facts our faith is founded on, verifying the gospel became largely a matter of our own experience.

We can see this in the words of some gospel songs that have little to do with the gospel itself: "He lives within my heart," "Love lifted me," and "Since I have been redeemed." Religious television and Christian magazines and biographies also often confuse the gospel with someone's experience of it.

Our risk of being taken in by a cult is compounded because we often define spirituality on the basis of such individual elements as devotions, prayer, evangelism, and Bible study rather than the whole of our lives. We are to live our total lives obediently before Christ—in our families, jobs, thoughts, prayers, evangelism, and relationships.

Spiritual leading. Evangelicals are easily manipulated by anything that hints at spirituality. One of our most popular statements is "The Lord led me."

At first, this sounds very spiritual, but it is seldom used in Scripture. On occasion, however, it is used to deceive. In 1 Kings 13, a false prophet deceived a man of God with such a phrase. Jacob did the same with Isaac (Genesis 27:20).

God does lead us, but these words are often overused.

One spring at Gordon College I received more than 20 letters from musical group leaders, pastors, and evangelists who had been "led of the Lord" to minister in New England during the first half of October, the peak of the fall colors. But God never seems to lead ministers to New England in February.

If all these people were truly led, then Gordon College should have canceled classes for a week in October to hold 20 chapel services.

All cultic leaders and churches that became cultic placed a high emphasis on being "led by the Lord." Our own misuse of this term can make us prey to cultic tendencies. And it can become a tool to manipulate others or to avoid responsibility for the decisions God places before us. To misuse it can border on taking God's name in vain.

Idealism and legalism. Evangelicals also tend toward legalism in our definitions of spirituality. Because our churches never live up to our expectations of the ideal spiritual church, we can become frustrated with them.

We can then be attracted to situations that promise or offer a more nearly perfect spiritual community. We can forget that "perfect" communities can come about at the expense of truth or freedom.

We often look to the New Testament church as our model Christian community, but it was not an ideal church. It had doctrinal and racial problems. On occasions, it overlooked sexual abuse and struggled with legalism. In one case it abused the Communion service with drunkenness.

Perhaps we should read Scripture before we boast of being another "New Testament church." And we must be careful not to adhere more legalistically to the ways of the New Testament church than we do to the gospel.

Evangelicals also tend to yoke our definitions of spirituality with certain cultural convictions. For many, these "don'ts," which are ignored or barely mentioned in Scripture, become more important than moral issues and commandments clearly presented in God's Word.

This kind of perspective has made many Christians vulnerable to cults. Most cults hold to "evangelical" convictions against the use of tobacco and alcohol and other worldly habits. They offer familiar but more intense group commitment. This gives a sense of security on the surface, but not a security rooted in God's Word and grace.

Here are some practical guidelines for dealing with subjective standards and legalism:

1. Be cautious when you hear "The Lord led me."

2. Learn to listen intently to a sermon and reflect on its content. Resist responding to emotional stories; instead, ask if they clarify the passage. We can evaluate a speaker's words by Scripture, but there are no such checks and balances concerning emotions.

3. Check that Scripture passages are used in their correct context.

4. Evaluate whether you get upset over Christians who do something you do not approve of culturally. Do you also condemn gossip, exaggeration, or other clear violations of Scripture?

5. Consider how you define spirituality. Is it in terms of devotions, or in terms of living under the authority of Christ and His Word?

Expectations of an Ideal Pastor

I often receive job descriptions from churches seeking pastors. Some of their expectations might as well require that he take yearly mission trips to Africa without the aid of a boat or plane!

A man who fills all the expectations of an ideal pastor risks being the main focus of the church. Recently two large evangelical churches, one on the East Coast and the other on the West, were granted loans for new sanctuaries with the stipulation that the pastor promise to stay for an extended period.

This indicates the direction our churches are taking. Almost every large, successful church or parachurch is built around a single individual. We seem to want a dynamic personality to be our authority figure.

About 15 years ago I had contact with a youth missions organization in Europe. On arrival, each team member was given a "victory sheet" that said never to question those in authority or write anything negative to those at home. This certainly is not the biblical model.

We seem to long for a successful, bionic pastor whose church can market him in a cassette ministry. Unfortunately, bionic people are half machine. Unlike Scripture, their biographies tell only of successes and ideal images to be followed. Such images of perfection border on idolatry.

This attitude toward a pastor can make our churches resemble cults more than we would like to think. Most cult leaders exude charisma and personality. They seem to be the ideal pastor in the ideal church.

And like members of cults, evangelicals can have difficulty admitting our own sins because we desire to be the ideal. We tend to justify our behavior, spiritualize it, or blame the church structure.

Inability to deal with our own sins and weaknesses, coupled with our vision for the ideal, makes us vulnerable to cultic-type leaders who give the image of successful and sinless leadership.

These guidelines may help us deal with the unspoken leadership expectations we may hold:

1. Keep in mind that all people of authority in Scripture were vulnerable to sin. Moses struck the rock; David needed Nathan's confrontation; and even after Pentecost, Peter needed Paul's rebuke.

2. Ask to whom your pastor is accountable. Can your

pastor deal with his weaknesses, and does he know his limitations?

3. Remember John's words, "If we claim to be without sin, we deceive ourselves and the truth is not in us" (1 John 1:8).

4. Remember that Christian biographies are written with marketing in mind. They often tell only one side, but the Bible is frank about difficulties in the lives of God's leaders.

5. Know that the purpose of the Body of Christ is to equip us for a better ministry. None of us has arrived yet. Even your own pastor, popular evangelists, and media preachers may be vulnerable to manipulative tactics and exaggerations.

The Danger of Guidance

Both evangelicals and cults place tremendous emphasis on guidance. Many cults favor group choice over personal choice or emphasize choices aided by a shepherd, leader, spiritual parent, or discipler.

Although many exciting things are happening with discipleship in evangelical churches, there are some dangers of abuse. Many current evangelical trends toward shepherding and discipling encourage having the leader make decisions for you.

Cultic leaders often build their systems for guidance and authority on Bible verses taken out of context. Many of our churches also emphasize one aspect of Scripture, excluding the rest.

The result is that some churches are built on body life, but lack in worship; others are built on discipleship, but fail to allow diversity. Some are based on evangelism, prophecy, or misuse in Scripture.

This can lead to an identity of opposition to the rest of the Body of Christ and move us out from under the authority of all of Scripture. Almost every cult began with an approach to Scripture that focused on one aspect of the Bible to the exclusion of the rest.

These pointers can help you keep decision-making practices in their proper perspective:

1. On Judgment Day, your shepherd or spiritual parent will not be there to give an account for you.

2. The Bible is not a book of magic promises that can be pulled out of context. A single verse is not always a complete thought. All promises, even ones we pull from our promise boxes, must be seen in the context of its passage. "I can do all things through Christ" (Philippians 4:13, KJV) is written in the context of Paul's saying he is content amid success or failure.

3. If all the teaching you receive is founded on just one aspect of God's truth, you are at high risk of becoming cultic. Paul declared "all the counsel of God" (Acts 20:27, KJV). Seek balance in your church.

The Danger of Group Sharing

Both cult members and evangelicals place a high emphasis on sharing. But when the sharing of our deep personal concerns is raised to a sign of spiritual maturity, we can move toward a cultic group mentality.

Sharing for the sake of sharing can easily lead to group manipulation, exploitation, and autocratic control. Cults, like evangelicals, emphasize devotions, evangelism, self-denial, sharing, and prayer as outward signs of spirituality.

When sharing, be mindful of these points:

1. In Scripture, secret sins are always dealt with secretly. In the Sermon on the Mount, Christ warns us to go into the closet to pray, not to come out of it (Matthew 6:6). The Psalmist says he couldn't share his despair with others without harming them (73:15). Jesus tells us that if someone has wronged us, we should confront him privately (Matthew 18:15). Likewise, in Scripture, public sins were dealt with publicly—as Paul dealt with Peter (Galatians 2:11).

2. Sharing is abused when it becomes a subtle way of gossiping.

3. Protect others' privacy. If a friend is having difficulty, ask his permission before sharing his needs with the group.

4. The Bible tells us to confess our sins, not our neighbor's, to one another (James 5:16).

The Danger of Independence

Cults see themselves as independent. They offer both uniformity and identity by their opposition to other groups.

Many of our evangelical churches were also established as a reaction—to liberalism or after a split from a church that didn't emphasize what we felt should be emphasized.

Evangelicals rarely belong to a church with a tradition of authority. Instead we tend to pride ourselves on our independence.

But of whom are we independent—God, Christ, the rest of the Body of Christ? "The eye cannot say to the hand, 'I don't need you!'" (1 Corinthians 12:21).

We can possibly even identify with an apparently Christian cult in our efforts to oppose a church we're dissatisfied with. Our own independent attitudes make it easy for us always to be looking for a community that promises something better or superior to the one we are presently in.

Coupled with this independence is our confusion between unity and uniformity. We often long for uniformity: Baptist with Baptists, high church with high churches, charismatic with charismatics, and free church with free churches. We seek out those who will reinforce our own likes and dislikes.

The result is a blindness to the richness of diversity God offers us within the Body of Christ, as well as a blindness to our own tendencies to write off the other members of the Body of Christ. We subtly remove our responsibility to "love one another" (John 13:35).

To counteract possible vulnerability to cults on this point, consider the following:

1. How much of your Christian identity is defined by opposition to liberals, Baptists, charismatics, etc.?

2. If you call yourself "independent," define the term in the light of 1 Corinthians 12:12-21.

3. Remember the New Testament church was diverse. Would you be willing to sing, "We are different in the Spirit"?

4. Choose to build relationships with Christians who come from different backgrounds. For example, if you are a Baptist, get to know a few charismatics; if you are a Nazarene, consciously build relationships with an Episcopalian.

Evangelicals are seldom drawn to cults because of beliefs or doctrine, but because in one of these areas the cults offer something more. If we think we are not vulnerable, then we are most vulnerable.

From *Unholy Devotion—Why Cults Lure Christians,* by Harold Bussell. © 1983, Zondervan Publishing Company, Grand Rapids. Reprinted by permission.

Chapter 10

Why Are There So Many Hypocrites in the Church?

by Stephen M. Miller

Background Scripture: Matthew 15:1-14; Acts 4:32—5:11

I'D RATHER GO TO CHURCH with a few hypocrites, than go to hell with them all" (Virginia Lea Ann Miller).

That's my mom talking.

She tossed me this pearl when I was a teenager, so fed up with hypocrisy in the church that I thought I'd gag. I wasn't ready to give up on Christianity, but I had already given up on our local church.

The problem was I had just been disillusioned by several of our practicing saints. And it had become incredibly clear to me that they needed much more practice. One of the women who worked with the youth was a particular disappointment. Through a series of events, I had discovered that with her busy mouth she had hurt several families in the church—mine included.

As far as I was concerned, there was no doubt her name belonged in *Webster's Dictionary*. Right beside **hyp-o-crite.**

Despite my disillusionment, along with the pain my whole family endured, we stayed in the same church. Mom and Dad both realized that wherever two or three are gathered in Christ's name, there's a real possibility a hypocrite snuck in.

In fact, that is the answer to the question: why are there so many hypocrites in the church? It's because we throw open the doors, and let any Thomas, Richard, and Harold walk right in and sit right down. There's no such thing as a hypocrite detector, and even if there were, we probably wouldn't use it. For of all the types of people who need the Lord, the hypocrite has to be in the top 10.

Potshots at Hypocricy

No one likes a hypocrite. Not even a hypocrite likes a hypocrite. That's why the Pharisees got mad when Jesus said, "You hypocrites! Isaiah was right when he prophesied about you: 'These people honor me with their lips, but their hearts are far from me'" (Matthew 15:7-8).

For as long as we humans have been recording words, we've been cursing hypocrites and their black art. Here are just a few of the memorable quotations on the matter.

Hypocrite: the man who murdered both his parents . . . [then] pleaded for mercy on the grounds he was an orphan.
Abraham Lincoln

A hypocrite is the kind of politician who would cut down a redwood tree, then mount the stump and make a speech for conservation. *Adlai E. Stevenson*

A bad man is worse when he pretends to be a saint.
Francis Bacon

No man, for any considerable period, can wear one face to himself, and another to the multitude, without finally getting bewildered as to which may be the true.
Nathaniel Hawthorne

> When you see a man with a great deal of religion displayed in his shop window, you may depend upon it he keeps a very small stock of it within.　　　*C. H. Spurgeon*

Bad-mouthing hypocrisy is easy. Not so easy, however, is trying to identify what exactly is hypocrisy.

The problem is we don't use the word *hypocrisy* the way Jesus used it.

Hypocrisy: What Modern Critics Say About It

When we call someone a hypocrite today, we're accusing him of pretending to be better than he really is.

And we immediately think of some extreme examples. Like the married pastor who ran off with the church secretary, after having had an affair with her for two years.

This may or may not fit Jesus' definition of hypocrisy, as we'll see in a bit. But if we take the modern definition of hypocrisy further, beyond this extreme example, we'll discover that the church is chock-full of hypocrites—for every breathing body in the place is an actor on the stage of hypocrisy. After all, who does not pretend to be better than he is? Don't we all put on our best behavior when we go out into the public? And don't we try to look as physically attractive as we can? But in hiding our weaknesses, and failures, and bumps, and moles, aren't we pretending to be better than we really are?

Oh. Well that's taking the definition too far, you say. It's natural to be on our best behavior in public. And it's perfectly acceptable to want to look physically attractive. There's nothing hypocritical about these.

And, of course, you're right. But this illustrates the truth that our modern definition needs a sharper focus.

Besides doing a little refocusing of the definition, we need to take a look at the modern hypocrite spotter. Sometimes this critic has the right and even the obligation to speak out.

In 1 Corinthians 5:1-12, Paul instructed the church to expel from membership the immoral man who was living in incest. He was sleeping with his father's wife. We don't know if this was the man's stepmother or his natural mother. But in either case, this was a blatant sin that needed a response from the local church. If this man was professing to be a Christian, as the passage certainly implies, then he was a hypocrite by all definitions—both modern and biblical.

These critics had every reason to isolate this man as a hypocrite. For they were asking no more of him than Scripture clearly taught. But modern critics of the church, including Christian critics within the church, are not always on such solid ground. Sometimes their expectations of Christians are greater than even Christ's expectations.

This can happen, for example, when a fundamentalist Christian confronts a liberal Christian.

I know of one church leader who insists that Christians in his flock follow some pretty rigid guidelines that outlaw things not specifically forbidden in the Bible. For example, he would view Christians as hypocrites if they wore jewelry —including wedding rings—or if they were women who wore slacks to church.

His rules are referred to by many Christians as "nonessentials" because the Bible does not clearly associate these with essentials to the Christian faith. This leader, however, justifies these rules on the grounds of what the Bible says about modesty and vanity.

What is interesting about this particular leader is that though he is concerned that his people not dress in such a way to call attention to themselves, he forever has a tan— even in the dead of winter. How can this be, since he lives in the snowbelt? Every morning while he stands before the mirror and goes through his routine of shaving, teeth brushing, and hair combing, he has a sun lamp blaring into his face.

To modern critics of the church, this fellow is a genuine, 10-karat hypocrite. A fake from his tanned hide to his narrow mind. What's ironic is that while preaching about the spiritual damage others are doing to themselves—because of vanity—he could be physically hurting himself for the same reason. Sun lamps can cause serious eye injury.

What about this church leader? Would Jesus have called him a hypocrite? Probably not. You see, Jesus reserved "hypocrite" for an elite troop of the unrighteous. He never used it to describe godly men and women. And despite the inconsistencies in this modern church leader, I'm convinced he is a Christian. In need of developing respect for the judgment of others, no doubt, but a Christian nonetheless.

I don't mean to excuse his inconsistency, for this sort of thing is bad news in today's church. It's the kind of thing non-Christians catch a glimpse of, magnify into church-wide proportions, then draw the conclusion that the church is no different from the rest of the world.

If this church leader is not the kind of hypocrite Jesus referred to, who is?

Hypocrisy: What Jesus Says About It

If you took some time to look up the background of the word *hypocrite* you would discover it is often associated with the ancient Greek theater.

And so, a lot of modern writers have tagged onto that idea to say that Jesus was referring to "play-actors." This seems to work well, since the Greek and Roman actors of Christ's time wore large masks and billowy costumes designed to increase the size of their appearance. And the idea is even more attractive when you consider that the actors wore platform shoes to make themselves taller, and that they exaggerated their gestures.

The parallel seems clear enough, since hypocrites want to be seen as bigger than life—as better than they really are.

But it's not that simple. If you look at the cases in which Jesus used the word, you discover that for Him, "hypocrite" is more closely related to the word's use in the Old Testament than to its use in the theater. In the King James Version, *hypocrite* appears 31 times. The Old Testament word refers to a person without piety, one who is godless.

The Pharisees that Jesus criticized with His harshest words in the New Testament were not simply inconsistent church leaders who were pretending to be better than they were. They rewrote the book on righteousness and lived by the minutiae of their own lawbook.

You see, they took the scores of commandments in the first five books of the Bible, then added hundreds more. It eventually got to the point where the rank and file Jews couldn't keep up with the ever-growing list of rules. But the Pharisees did—and they prided themselves in obeying each of the rules. The masses, too, seemed to admire these church leaders for their dedication.

In a way, the Pharisees were like actors who played to the crowd. They followed all the rules, as everyone could see. But they were doing that which *they* defined as good. As a result, with their preoccupation on trees they missed the forest. They kept the unimportant rules, like not carrying a load more than two yards on the Sabbath, but ignored the principles behind the rules—principles designed to help us love God with all our heart and to love others as ourselves.

Oh, they gave their tithe. They prayed and fasted. They taught Jewish boys about the Law and the history of God at work in the nation. But their effort to impress people perverted all of their service. And their self-righteousness—the confidence they had in their own goodness because of their service—blocked any attempts, by God and man, to convince them of their hypocrisy.

For Jesus, a hypocrite is not a flawed man of God. A hypocrite is not even an average Christian pretending to be above average.

A hypocrite is someone who claims to love God, but who has turned away from God. Instead of serving the Lord, he serves himself and the fallen angel who has become the god of selfishness.

In Christ's time as today, hypocrites are the blind leading the blind. And both are doomed.

Remember Ananias and Sapphira of the Early Church? They wanted to be seen as spiritual leaders in this new religious movement. We read in Acts 4:32-37 that a man named Barnabas received public acclaim for selling a field and giving the money to the apostles, to be used to help the needy.

Ananias and Sapphira decided to do the same—not because of the need but because of the potential acclaim. According to the way we use *hypocrisy* today, this pair met the job description. But we really can't say for certain if they were the kind of ungodly people Jesus referred to. If God actually struck them down, as many interpret Acts 5:1-11, they probably were a couple devils beneath plastic halos. But for all we know, they were just confused Christians who died of shock when the truth was revealed.

So What?

Who cares if they, or anyone else for that matter, are hypocrites according to today's definition but not according to the definition Jesus used?

As Christians in the church, we need to see the patience Jesus had with "saints in process"—the ones we're inclined to call hypocrites. To disciples who failed Him, like Peter ... to religious leaders who wanted to grow beyond their weaknesses ... to righteous men and women of the day who wrestled with sins that forever buffet humanity—to all these people, He expressed compassion, He modeled love, and He urged them on to holiness.

We make a big mistake when we isolate struggling or misguided Christians, then blast them with all the intensity

Jesus blasted the Pharisees. To the growing Christian, we need to provide small doses of truth—in quantities they can respond to—along with overdoses of love.

To the modern Pharisees—those who are blatant in their disregard of the clear essentials of the Christian faith, but who call themselves Christians par excellence—we need to treat them with all the holy but firm rebuke required for spiritually blind people who are leading the blind.

To modern critics of the church, we must admit that as long as humans have anything to do with worship, there will be struggling Christians whose lives don't always measure up to the biblical requirements. And there will always be the ungodly who wear the garb of Christianity, and who speak the language, but whose lives reveal the person beneath the costume and behind the memorized lines.

But there is good news, too. It's that where two or three are gathered to worship the Lord, most of the folk are sincere believers who love God with all their heart and their neighbors as themselves. And even better news is that where two or three are gathered, Jesus is there, too.

And after all, the truth of Christianity does not depend on the faithfulness of a species famous for its spiritual weakness, but on the faithfulness of Christ. When we look to others for spiritual truth and consistent living, we will sometimes be disappointed, disillusioned, and discouraged. But Jesus will never fail us.

Stephen M. Miller is electives editor for Church of the Nazarene Headquarters, Kansas City.

Chapter 11

How Do We Know Jesus Was Resurrected?

by Rod Huron

Background Scripture: Matthew 28:1-20

Do YOU GO TO CEMETERIES very often? There's one here in town where you can find as many joggers as dead people. Well, almost as many. Some people do go to cemeteries to jog, or to enjoy the stillness, or to see the trees and flowers. But the usual reason is none of these.

Most people go to graveyards to pay their respects to those whose bodies lie buried there. I remember rounding a bend late one afternoon and coming upon a young man bending over a freshly made grave. Hoping he had not seen me, I changed direction and jogged down another way. When I came back he was gone.

I couldn't help going over to see.

At the foot of the grave, almost buried by the wilted flowers, was a little metal stand holding a cardboard marker with the name and date. The body was that of a girl, probably his wife, 22, buried less than three weeks.

Yes, people return to the burial places of their loved ones so they can feel close to them.

In Jesus' case this is impossible.

His body isn't here. You can't go to the place where His body is buried. It isn't here.

Did you get that?

Jesus' tomb is empty.

The body is gone.

Where Did the Body Go?

Jesus was not tried in secret and shot in a cellar. His trial was a noisy affair, with shouted accusations, a crowd, soldiers, a lengthy procession to the place of execution, and death not coming until long hours of public exposure and shame.

On Pentecost when Peter spoke of Jesus' trial and crucifixion, no one had to ask, "Which Jesus?" Everybody knew.

His death was public; His burial scarcely less so.

Joseph of Arimathea was a rich and prominent member of the Sanhedrin, respected as "a good and upright man" (Luke 23:50). Nicodemus, too, was a member of this ruling body (John 7:50).

Here were two of the nation's leaders, comparable to our senators, perhaps, claiming the body from Governor Pilate. Surprised that Jesus had died so soon, Pilate sent for the centurion and questioned him to be sure (Mark 15:44).

No ordinary grave for Jesus. Joseph placed the body in his own new tomb, the one he had commissioned to be chiseled out of solid rock. Only the rich could afford such. The tomb had only recently been completed and fortunately was close to the place of death (John 19:41).

Neither man spared expense. For burial wrapping, Joseph bought linen. Nicodemus' contribution was a hundred *litrai* (about 75 pounds) of myrrh and aloes to be placed about the body.

"The women," Luke tells us, "who had come with Jesus from Galilee followed Joseph and saw the tomb and how his body was laid in it" (Luke 23:55). Their closest friend was being laid to rest, and they had to see the place.

Nor were they the only ones interested in the proceedings. Remembering what Jesus had said, His accusers went to Pilate and arranged for a guard to be posted. Taking no chances, the soldiers secured the tomb and placed their seal on the stone door (Matthew 27:62-66). Can you think of any better way to make sure the body would *not* be stolen?

Before dawn on Sunday morning the women came to add their spices to those Nicodemus had provided. The events of that morning have been repeated to us so often that it is difficult for us to grasp their stunned reaction at finding the tomb opened and empty.

Mary runs to Peter and John. The other women see an angel, who tells them Jesus is risen. With mixed feelings of fear and joy, they hurry off to tell the disciples.

Peter and John come running, John reaching the tomb first. He looks in but stands outside. Then Peter comes and goes in, and John follows.

By now the terror-stricken guards have reached the authorities, setting off another reaction. The authorities hold a conference and put out a cover story.

Reports begin to come that different ones have seen Jesus: Mary Magdalene, some other women, Simon Peter. It is a bewildered group that comes together that evening, made even more bewildered when the men from Emmaus burst in, saying they have seen Him and He has gone home with them.

Accusation: The Disciples Stole the Body

Search carefully. Go back over every inch of ground; dissect every conversation. Whatever else the disciples are doing, they're not sitting around saying, "Hey, guys, what do we do with this body we stole?"

Yet this is precisely what they were accused of doing.

> When the chief priests had met with the elders and devised a plan, they gave the soldiers a large sum of money, telling them, "You are to say, 'His disciples came during the night and stole him away while we were asleep.' If this report gets to the governor, we will satisfy him and keep you out of trouble." So the soldiers took the money and did as they were instructed. And this story has been widely circulated among the Jews to this very day.
>
> —Matthew 28:12-15

How did the disciples get away with that body? Did all 11 help with it? Or was it supposed that only one or two did the deed?

Did Peter take Jesus' body? That coward! He was so afraid that he let a little servant girl scare a denial out of him. Would stealing have given him the courage to stand before a crowd and announce that Jesus had risen from the dead? And do it so effectively that 3,000 were convinced and turned to Christ?

Did Thomas? Doubter, a twin, knowing how people could mistake identity. OK, Thomas, suppose you stole the body. What for? So you could be sure you knew where Jesus was? Then what? You wouldn't believe even when they started telling you that He had come back. Would you have let them go on saying He was alive if you knew He was still dead?

Maybe John took the body. John stayed closest when Jesus was on trial, closest when He was on the Cross. Maybe John couldn't think of parting with Jesus and crept past the guards, forced the door open, shouldered the body onto his back and struggled off with it.

Where would he take it? He had no home in Jerusalem: he was a Galilean. Corpses have a way of announcing their presence most forcefully. Especially in warm climates.

If they had the body—one of them, or two or three, or all of them together—if they had the body, how do we account for their heroic courage in the face of intense and increasing opposition? Did they risk their lives for a story they knew to be a lie?

Accusation: Someone Else Took the Body

Maybe someone else took it and did not tell the disciples. Maybe Joseph decided he wanted his tomb back, so he came and took the body out.

How did he get by the soldiers? And where did he put the body?

Maybe the women did it. Maybe they took the body outside so they could finish their embalming in the daylight.

Then why didn't they put it back? Surely they couldn't afford a better tomb. And then there were the soldiers.

Or maybe someone else took it.

Did the soldiers? Did Pilate? Did one of the chief priests? Or several of them working together? Or several Pharisees?

Do you think Jesus' enemies would have remained silent when Peter stood before a festival crowd and said Jesus was alive? Do you think they would have resorted to threats and beatings and prison and murder, trying to contain this spreading new faith, when all they had to do was produce the dead body of Jesus?

They did not produce the dead body because they could not! How His enemies wished they knew where the body was! Yet never one time did any of Jesus' attackers deny that His tomb was empty. At no time did a single voice say, "We know where the body is."

Jesus' body was not in Joseph's grave or any other grave. Jesus' body was alive again. He was working with His disciples, actively preparing them for the time when He would return to the Father and they would carry on His work.

Whoever took the body out of the tomb surely wasn't in much of a hurry. First they removed the head covering and folded it. Then they found a way to take the body but leave the burial cloth still lying where it was.

All this after they had shoved the door out of the way, of course. Ever try pushing a stone door?

Now all they needed to do was carry the body—if you've ever lifted someone who was unconscious or dead you know what that's like—and get away without being seen by the guards.

Once that was done, all they had to do was find a place to hide it. Yes, and keep absolutely silent when the apostles began telling everywhere that Jesus was alive again.

Do you believe that is what happened?

Accusation: The Women Went to the Wrong Tomb

If no one has the body, maybe it is still there someplace. Maybe Mary went to the wrong tomb. Maybe when she didn't find Jesus' body, she ran to the disciples with the tale, "Jesus is alive." Maybe Jesus' tomb was too difficult to find.

If that's true, then it must have been hard to find Golgotha too, because we know from someone who was there that the tomb was very close to the place Jesus was crucified (John 19:41-42). Besides, Mary had watched the burial (Mark 15:47). Can we believe she couldn't find the place again?

The tomb belonged to Joseph of Arimathea (Matthew 27:57-60). He claimed the body, and he and Nicodemus did the actual burying (John 19:38-42). Several women among Jesus' followers watched to see where He was buried, then went home and prepared spices and perfumes to use after the Sabbath was over. They took note of the place because they expected to come back. Do you think none of them remembered?

Do you think Joseph would forget where his own tomb was? Or Nicodemus, would he forget how to get back to the place he had helped bury Jesus?

That tomb was chiseled out of rock in a rich man's garden close to execution hill. They weren't trying to locate one of a dozen graves dug in flat ground.

Several years ago an unbeliever suggested that the women were crying so much that in their grief and tears they missed the right place, and a young man saw them and tried to tell them they were wrong: "He's not here; he is over there." Startled, the women ran off, hearing only the first part of the boy's message. Then they allowed their imaginations to go to work and told the disciples Jesus had been raised from the dead.

Is that what you think happened?

If you were Joseph of Arimathea and someone told you that a body you had put in your own cemetery had come back to life, what would you do? Don't you think you might go down and check it out?

Is Nicodemus going to sit still while Jerusalem is ablaze with talk of Jesus' resurrection? No, he is going to go and see whether that body is still where he and Joseph put it. And if it is, do you think he is going to keep silent?

Accusation: Jesus Wasn't Really Dead

Every now and then someone offers the possibility that Jesus had carefully planned His "death" and "resurrection." For example, one theory suggests that as He cried "I thirst," a confederate slipped Him a powerful drug that induced unconsciousness, signaling His disciples to run to Pilate for permission to take Him down. This done, Jesus spent the next couple of days recuperating, and on Sunday "rose again."

They overlook all that happened before and during Jesus' crucifixion.

Scourging was a terrible punishment. Jewish law forbade more than 40 lashes, but the Romans showed no mercy. Victims sometimes died under the whip.

His back raw, His scalp and forehead lacerated, bruises on His body, Jesus was stretched across two rough-hewn timbers while nails were pounded through His hands and feet. Thus fastened, He was raised aloft to hang in increasing pain and exhaustion.

When His body finally sagged unmoving, His followers thought He died. The soldiers thought He died. The centurion, charged with putting the prisoners to death, thought He died. Taking no chances, he speared the body to be sure. The centurion would forfeit his life if he were mistaken.

John, standing close enough to see it all, thought Jesus was dead. The executioners thought Jesus was dead. The priests thought Jesus was dead. Pilate thought Jesus was dead. The guards posted at the tomb thought He was dead.

Putting on an act? Some kind of drug? Fainting spell? Every person there would scoff at the idea.

So would those who saw Jesus after His resurrection. A person who had experienced what Jesus went through would need sympathy and care three days later, yet Mary Magdalene offers none. Instead, she falls at His feet in worship.

The women, suddenly meeting Jesus, do the same.

The two travelers on their way to Emmaus don't suspect that their companion has been tied to a post and brutally whipped three days before; worse, that He has been nailed to a cross. Weren't they walking? And wasn't it seven miles?

When Jesus, that same evening, displays His wounds to the disciples, they don't see swollen flesh, tender and painful. The marks are there, but those hands and feet will never hurt again.

Jesus doesn't talk like someone fighting fever and loss of blood. With assurance and power He points them to the waiting world, and tells how they will go everywhere in His name.

Didn't really die? That accusation simply doesn't fit.

Accusation: The Disciples Only Thought They Were Seeing Jesus

The priests and Pharisees were malicious in their accusation that the disciples stole the body. Others try to be more kind, saying, "No, we aren't accusing the disciples of lying. It is just that they were mistaken. They thought they were seeing Jesus."

They thought they were seeing a ghost. Jesus showed them His hands and feet and talked with them, but that wasn't enough. Then He asked if they had anything to eat (Luke 24:36-43). They were not easy to convince.

Nor was Thomas. He demanded proof. Jesus gladly submitted to the very test Thomas proposed. If Thomas' doubts went beyond the others', so did His response. When Jesus showed His hands and side, Thomas cried out, "My Lord and my God!" (John 20:24-28). He could not possibly doubt any longer.

Is the resurrection of Jesus only hallucination? Did the disciples manufacture the risen Christ out of their own shattered hopes? Look at it again. Where is the evidence that a single one of them expected Him to come back? They were crushed, their dreams broken.

When reports started coming that Jesus was alive again, they didn't believe them. "Their words seemed to them like nonsense" (Luke 24:11). Thomas refused to believe his fellow apostles! On the mountain in Galilee as Jesus was preparing to issue the Great Commission, some in that crowd still doubted (Matthew 28:17).

We hear from those who deny that Jesus' body came from the grave that it was only a "spiritual" resurrection. That may be one half-inch removed from the "vision" theory, but it is equally false.

If Jesus' body still lies in Palestine, He runs a poor third behind Enoch and Elijah, who were spared death. Perhaps we ought to look to one of them for hope in a life to come. Not even an unbeliever would suggest that!

Accusation: The Records Are Not Reliable

Handling our leather-bound New Testaments, with their pages edged in gold, we sometimes forget that here are firsthand records of eyewitnesses.

Matthew was one of the Twelve. Mark was closely associated with Simon Peter (Acts 12:1-17; 1 Peter 5:13). Luke "carefully investigated everything from the beginning" (Luke 1:3). John personally examined the empty tomb and talked many times with Jesus after the Resurrection (John 20:3—21:25).

Scholars have documented passages from New Testament books quoted in other writings of that era and traced the records back to the very days of the apostles. Paul speaks of over 500 witnesses to the Resurrection, most of them still living at the time he wrote (1 Corinthians 15:6).

We are not looking at a fable made up long afterward and circulated among gullible illiterates.

Accusation: The Records Are Full of Contradictions

Three years ago I had an automobile accident. I had pulled out onto an icy street, was exceeding the 25-mile speed limit. I saw a trailer-truck hauling coal coming toward me, which I thought I recognized. I glanced up to see who was driving, and suddenly a big crew-cab pulled out from behind the truck and blocked the road.

When the lady driving the crew-cab saw me, she froze. By that time I had hit the brakes and was sliding toward her. She screamed, the older woman on the passenger side was yelling, and in slow motion I went right into her truck.

Her husband came running out of the house, and I got out and went across the street to call the Highway Patrol.

In court she testified that she remembered no truck passing her house, but she thought I was driving too fast. Her husband did not see the truck, and neither did her son, who was in the front yard. However, another eyewitness testified that there was a truck. I had the driver's name, but he was not called to testify, as he did not see the crash. My testimony was different from that of the other driver, and other eyewitnesses also gave different testimony. Does that imply that there never was a collision between my car and her crew-cab?

The judge didn't think so. Taking all the evidence into consideration, he was able to reconstruct the total picture, assigning 80 percent of the responsibility to her and 20 percent to me.

Matthew gives us information not found in John, and Luke tells us about things we don't get from the others. Does that mean there was no Resurrection? Does it mean the records are not accurate in what they do tell?

What do you think?

It is by combining the data given by all of these four independent witnesses that we complete our understanding of what took place.

John Fitzgerald Kennedy, 35th President of the United States, died when struck in the head by a shot from a 6.5 Mannlicher-Carcano rifle. He was attended by Dr. Malcolm Perry, Surgeon Charles James, and others. Attempts at resuscitation failed, and Kennedy lies buried at Arlington National Cemetery, Washington, D.C.

Jesus of Nazareth died on a cross during a Jewish feast, in the presence of the disciple John, His mother Mary, and others. Three days later they saw Him alive again.

Kennedy and Jesus both died in real places, were seen and cared for by real people. Both were buried in real cemeteries. But there the similarity ends.

Kennedy still lies at Arlington.

And where do you think Jesus is?

From *Say Hello to Life,* Rod Huron. © 1985, The Standard Publishing Company, Cincinnati, Ohio. Division of Standex International Corporation. Reprinted by permission.

Chapter 12

Isn't Hell Just a Scare Tactic?

by D. James Kennedy

Background Scripture: Matthew 13:24-30, 36-43; Mark 9:42-48

HELL. There is not a subject in the world so repugnant to the human mind as this one, yet no subject is of greater importance.

Jesus wept when He contemplated the destruction of Jerusalem. God himself says, "I take no pleasure in the death of the wicked" (Ezekiel 33:11). No Christian can find joy in the contemplation of the final abode of the impenitent. However, it is our duty as faithful ministers of Jesus Christ to proclaim the whole message of God. I believe I would be a false friend to any sinner if I did not warn him, as the Scriptures repeatedly do, of the danger of his condition.

It is a well-known fact that people suppress what they hate and fear. Consequently there are numerous persons who, instead of seriously considering the matter of hell, simply castigate the one who brings it to their attention. Though a minister may have half a dozen degrees, he is still

railed upon as an obscurantist who is to be ignored if he preaches on the subject. I have found that the arguments of unbelievers consist of one thing: emotionalism displayed in an outburst of hostility and unwillingness to consider rationally a matter of the greatest importance to their eternal well-being.

Some people seem to be under the delusion that hell has evaporated, or at least that all intelligent people have stopped believing in it. Before continuing in any such ideas, I ask you to consider these words of the great Princeton theologian, A. A. Hodge: "The Old Testament was in the hands of the Jews centuries before Christ came. They uniformly understood these Scriptures as teaching that the wicked are to suffer forever." The first-century Jewish historian Josephus declares that this was also the understanding of the Pharisees of his time. As Christians we have had Scriptures for almost 20 centuries. We read that "all the great church fathers, Reformers, and historical churches, with their recensions and translations of the Sacred Scriptures, their liturgies and hymns; all the great evangelical theologians and biblical scholars, with their grammars, dictionaries, commentaries, and classical systems, have uniformly agreed in their understanding of the teaching of the Sacred Scriptures as to the endlessness of the future sufferings of all who die impenitent. And this has come to pass against the universal and impetuous current of human fears and sympathies."[1]

The Bible tells us that the unbeliever will go into endless punishment. Is that contrary to what any rational, right-thinking person would conclude from what we know of God? By no means! Joseph Stiles points out to us that the laws of our nature demand that there be a hell: "Fix your eye upon the very vilest sinner upon earth. Through death, this instant, pass him up to Heaven—with all his lusts, and lies, and hate, and devilish heart—can he be happy there? By a law of his nature, happiness lies in a correspondence between the mind and its subject. By another law of his nature, misery lies in the opposition between the mind and its object. This unholy heart feels, and must ever feel, the deepest aversion to everything that exists or transpires in holy Heaven."[2]

Our own moral nature requires such a place as hell. The human conscience also demands it. All men feel that there is a difference between virtue and vice and that in character these are moral opposites. And always we treat them as such: we approve virtue and condemn vice. We reward virtue to promote it, and punish vice to suppress it. This is also true in all moral governments of any moral nation—laws have been passed because people know that virtue leads to happiness of the community.

We see another argument from the life of Jesus Christ and His character. Christ, who came meek and mild to save us from pain and suffering, was the One who talked more about hell than any other person in Scripture. Did this One who is truth incarnate, who is the Holy Son of God, come to implant in the minds of men a fear that would last for over 19 centuries, of something that is nonexistent? Such a thought is a great smear upon the character of Jesus Christ. Some people say: "But God is love! And God will never punish anyone in hell." It is very dangerous to erect a doctrine on an inaccurate premise. Indeed the Bible does teach us that God is love, infinitely compassionate love. But the same Bible teaches us that the same God is holy and just and righteous; that He is of purer eyes than to look upon iniquity, and that He will visit our transgressions with the rod and our iniquity with stripes; that He will by no means clear the guilty.

Long before the love of God was fully manifested in the Scripture, the one great thought that saturated the minds of the Hebrew people was: "Holy, holy, holy is the Lord Almighty" (Isaiah 6:3). The very foundation of His throne was holiness, and no sin would ever come into His presence without His inevitably consuming it with His wrath.

There are those who would have us believe that they know something about God that we do not know, and therefore this could not be the case. The Universalist declares that God, in His love, must inevitably receive everyone. This person would tell us that God does not quite understand himself and surely does not mean what He says and actually is gravely mistaken about this matter. But throughout all of revelation, from Genesis to the end, God declared that the wicked will die in their sins and not find peace. The Scripture says that God's ways are not our ways and His thoughts are not our thoughts (Isaiah 55:8); that His ways and thoughts are past finding out (Romans 11:33). Nevertheless, this blasphemer confidently declares that God's ways *are* our ways and His thoughts *are* our thoughts, and that He has fully found out God's ways. This man would bring upon himself the exclamation of God who has said, "You thought I was altogether like you" (Psalm 50:21). He is the Holy God, who has declared that He will not sanction sin. The impenitent thrust themselves into His presence with great folly and with endless consequences.

Others have said, "Surely our sins would not deserve such a thing as endless punishment." Another author has said to us that the end of punishment for our sins must be when the influence of these sins ceases. But if the influence of men's sins live through all time, then men are accountable for those influences through all time. Man cannot but be punished in proportion to his guilt until time be no more.

The Scriptures state that if the effects of our sins are everlasting then the punishment for our sins will also be everlasting. The main reason we believe in hell is because Jesus Christ declares that it is so. We are told that the sinner dwells in "everlasting burning" (Isaiah 33:14), yet "will never see the light" (Psalm 49:19); is "destroyed, completely" (Psalm 73:19), yet "the fire is not quenched" (Mark 9:44); is everlastingly "dead" (Isaiah 26:14), the "worm [in him] does not die" (Mark 9:44), is torn "to pieces with no one to rescue" (Psalm 7:2); when he calls, he is never answered; when he seeks he never finds. In a word, he sinks to a death beyond prayer, a condemnation beyond forgiveness, and a doom beyond the reach of Christ.

One author has stated that every Hebrew and Greek word used to describe the eternality of the existence of God and the eternality of the blessedness of the redeemed in heaven is also used to describe the eternality of the sufferings of the lost in hell.[3] If the punishment of the wicked is temporal, then there will come a day when God will be extinct, because the same terms are used.

William Munsey describes to us something of the meaning of eternity, something which so often men thrust from their minds: "Eternity cannot be defined. Beginningless and endless it cannot be measured—its past increased, its future diminished. It has no past, it has no future, it has no ends, it has no middle, it has no parts—an unanalyzable, tremendous unity. If all the mountains of all the worlds were pressing upon the brain, they could not weigh it down more heavily than eternity's least conception ... It is unoriginated, beginningless, endless, measureless, imperishable, indescribable, undefinable thing. Itself is its only definition. If asked, What is eternity? we can only answer 'Eternity,' and in our answer confess our weakness and folly."[4]

When you have been in hell a hundred billion, trillion eons of centuries, you will not have one less second to be there—to be lost forever.

Where will you spend forever? Though the Scripture declares it in a thousand places, and Jesus boldly asserted that it was true, there may be some who still do not believe in hell. I have heard the testimony of a man who went to hell. He is a living man, and his testimony is on tape. He has given me his permission to use it in any way that I wish. He described himself as an atheist. He believed neither in soul nor spirit nor angel nor God. "When you are dead," he said, "you are dead like a dog." One day he planned to crawl into a hole and pull the top in over him. He did not believe in heaven or hell or God.

But then he did, in a very enlightening way—he died! Not long ago he had a cardiac arrest, and the doctors pronounced him clinically dead. (In the last year or so many scientists have reported on over 500 people who have been pronounced dead and have been resuscitated. Whatever that means, we may not wholly know, but the reports that they bring back have convinced scientists that there is life beyond death.) Later he was resuscitated, but he told me that during his "death" he experienced the following: He sank into a realm of darkness, a place of dark shadows—yet still he had a body. He found himself in great agony pushing a huge stone into a pit. (The Bible speaks of a pit.) He was in great pain and there was nothing he could do to diminish it.

"If you got shot in the arm," he said, "you could at least

grab your arm and get some slight lessening of pain, but not so with this."

I asked, "Where was it? Was it localized?"

His answer was, "No, it was everywhere. I am quite certain that if I had cut my throat I would not have lessened that pain at all."

When I questioned how severe the pain was, he said, "It was worse than anything I have ever experienced in this world."

I thought perhaps he had never known much pain. I asked, "Have you ever really suffered any pain in this world?"

He said, "When I was nine years old a freight train ran over my leg and left it hanging by a tendon. Somehow I picked it up, dragged myself to a crossing, and was finally picked up by a man in a car. I never passed out but my blood squirted all over his windshield as he drove me to a hospital. I was never unconscious."

"How did that pain compare to the time when the doctor said you were dead?" I asked.

"It was insignificant," he answered. "I wouldn't even compare it."

I told him, "I once burned my hand rather severely and experienced a pain unlike anything I have ever known before or since. Did you ever burn yourself?"

He said, "Yes, I knocked a can of gasoline off a shelf over a candle onto my leg and set my remaining leg on fire. As a result I spent several weeks in the hospital." He raised his pants leg and showed me the scars.

I said, "I know of nothing in this world that compares to the pain of burning. How did the pain you experienced when you died compare with that?"

He answer, "It was one thousand times worse than when my leg was on fire! I tried every way I knew to explain that away, but everything dissolved before my attempts to do it. I did not believe in hell before and I did not want to believe in it then. On the face of this earth, no matter what you did to me, I don't think you could experience the pain that I experienced in that hospital."

I asked, "What do you think that was?"

"Why, I feel that it definitely had to be something other than on this earth, so the only place I can think of is that there must be a hell, and I was in it." He told me that when he thought about that after he got out of the hospital, he began to tremble uncontrollably.

Hell is real! He believed it did not exist at all, just as some who are reading this believe. He thought it was a myth. He did not believe Christ. He did not believe God, he did not believe the Bible. But he died, and he believes it now! Tragically, some will only believe it when they experience it— when it will be too late.

If the Bible teaches anything at all, it is that there is an everlasting too late—that there will come a moment when it will be eternally too late, when the door of grace will have slammed shut forever. Then the sinner would give the universe itself for just one minute to repent and turn to Jesus Christ.

I believe there is a hell because Jesus Christ not only taught it, He experienced it. We read in the Scripture that on the Cross of Calvary, Christ took upon himself the sin of the world; he was made sin for us, and our guilt was imputed to him. God the Father looked down upon His beloved Son whom He had loved everlastingly, in whom He was well pleased, and saw Him as the Lamb of God that taketh away the sin of the world. And God poured out the caldron of His wrath against sin itself and it all poured out upon Jesus Christ who cried, "My God, my God, why have you forsaken me?" (Matthew 27:46), and then descended into hell.

In that darkness at noon Christ suffered an infinite penalty there upon the Cross in our place. He said, "It is finished. It is paid." Those who will trust in Him can hear His words that the wages of sin, though it is death, is paid forever by Christ. And those who place their trust in Him have His word that they will never perish. The truth of the Scripture is that the anger and wrath of God will one day fall upon our sins. The only question is: Will it fall upon us in hell forever? Or will it fall upon Jesus Christ upon the Cross? That choice is ours to make. We will live forever—somewhere.

1. A. A. Hodge, *Popular Lectures on Theological Themes* (Philadelphia: Presbyterian Board of Publications, 1887), 456, 457.

2. Joseph C. Stiles, *Future Punishment* (St. Louis, Mo.: n.p., 1868), 4.

3. William Elbert Munsey, *Eternal Retribution* (Murfreesboro, Tenn: Sword of the Lord Publishers, 1951), 65.

4. Ibid., 62.

Condensed from "Why I Believe in Hell" in *Why I Believe,* by D. James Kennedy, copyright © 1980; used by permission of Word Books, Publisher, Waco, Tex.

Chapter 13

How Do I Know There's a Heaven?

by D. James Kennedy

Background Scripture: John 14:1-4; Revelation 21:1-4;
22:1-5

No QUESTION has plagued the minds of men and women
more continously and universally than the question raised
by Job so many centuries ago. "If a man die, shall he live
again?" (14:14, KJV).

Over 1,300 years ago in the portion of England known
as Northumbria, the first Christian missionaries arrived.
They came to the courts of King Edwin of Northumbria, and
in this great hall ablaze with the light of many torches, huge
logs in the fireplace, and grizzled chieftains surrounding
them, these Christian missionaries gave their first discourse
on the Christian faith.

When they had finished, one asked, "Can this new religion tell us anything of what happens after death? The soul
of man is like a sparrow flying through this lighted hall. It
enters at one door from the darkness outside, flits through
the light and warmth, and passes out at the further end into

the dark again. Can this new religion solve for us the mystery?"[1]

I, for one, am convinced that this new religion, now old with age, is the only one that can give us any sure and certain word concerning life after death. I believe in immortality; I believe in heaven. The reasons are manifold. Not all of them have the same weights in my mind or the minds of any other individuals, of course, but together they form the threads of what I believe is an exceedingly strong cord.

First of all, let us consider an argument from the realm of science. The first law of thermodynamics states that energy or matter cannot be created or destroyed. They may be transformed one into the other, but they cannot be destroyed. This was set forth by Einstein and was conclusively demonstrated at Hiroshima. Burris Jenkins put it this way: "No single atom in creation can go out of existence, according to the scientists; it only changes in form. We cannot burn up anything; we simply change it from a solid to a gaseous state. Neither is any energy or force ever destroyed; it is only changed from one form to another."[2] If man ceases to exist, he will be the only thing in this universe that does. Therefore, to begin with there is the probability that we shall continue to exist.

Second, let us consider this analogy from nature. It has probably never been stated any better than by William Jennings Bryan in his *Analogies of Nature:* "Christ gave us proof of immortality, and yet it would hardly seem necessary that one should rise from the dead to convince us that the grave is not the end. If the Father deigns to touch with divine power the cold and pulseless heart of the buried acorn and to make it burst forth into a new life, will He leave neglected in the earth the soul of man, made in the image of his Creator? If He stoops to give to the rosebush whose withered blossoms float upon the autumn breeze, the sweet assurance of another springtime, will He refuse the words of hope to the sons of men when the frosts of winter come? If matter, mute and inanimate, though changed by the forces of nature into a multitude of forms, can never die, will the spirit of man suffer annihilation when it has paid a brief visit like a royal guest to this tenement of clay? No, I am as sure that there is another life as I am that I live today!"[3]

Third, there is the universal longing of mankind for eternity. Some people may never have considered that such a longing does not exist in the breast of any part of the brute creation. In his book *After Death—What?* Dr. Madison C. Peters said: "The flocks and herds upon a thousand hills, the myriad forms of insect life, every winged fly and tuneful beetle, the fish that gaily sport and gambol in the rivers and seas, all can find the end of their being; not a thought of future want disturbs their perfect tranquillity. But never so with man. He only is never satisfied no matter what his wealth, or fame, or knowledge, or power, or earthly pleasures. From the king to the beggar, 'man never is, but always to be blest.'"[4]

What is the explanation? I believe the Scriptures give to us very clearly the fact that God has placed immortality—eternity—in the breast of man. This longing is found everywhere.

There has never been a race of men upon this earth—whether in the deepest heart of Africa, in the South Seas, or on the highest mountain that has not had a belief in some future life—whether it is the happy hunting grounds of the American Indians, some palace in the sky, some sensual abode of the Muslim.

This has been true not only of the brute savage, the superstitious and the ignorant, but of the greatest philosophical minds of history. Crito asked Socrates on the night of the latter's death: "But in what way would you have us bury you?" "In any way that you like," Socrates replied; "only you must get hold of me, and take care that I do not walk away from you." Plato, in his *Phaedon,* presents powerful arguments for a belief in immortality, as do the philosopher Schelling and others too numerous to be mentioned.[5]

Everywhere, from the Fiji Islands to the dens of the philosophers, it has been believed that man shall live on.

We have been made for eternity! Yet though such a belief exists in every ancient religion from the Egyptian to the Persian to the Assyrian and Babylonian, the Chinese and the Hindu, everywhere it has waited for Jesus Christ to give to it a certitude nothing else could grant.

Professor Adolf von Harnack said: "Christ's grave was the birthplace of an indestructible belief that death is vanquished and there is life eternal. It is useless to cite Plato; it is useless to point to the Persian religion and the ideas and literature of later Judaism. All that would have perished; but the certainty of the resurrection and of a life eternal which is bound up with the grave in Joseph's garden has not perished; and on the conviction that Jesus lives we still base those hopes of citizenship in an Eternal City which make our earthly life worth living and tolerable. He delivered them who, through fear of death, were all their lifetime subject to bondage."[6] "He is risen" is the certain and sure hope of all of those who trust in him. Not only do we have the universal testimony of mankind but we have the testimony of Jesus Christ and His resurrection.

Dr. Simon Greenleaf, the Royall Professor of Law at Harvard, one of the greatest authorities on legal evidence the world has ever known, turned the vast searchlight of his immense knowledge of evidences upon the evidence for the resurrection of Jesus Christ and exposed every thread of that evidence to the most searching criticism. He came to the conclusion that the evidence was so overwhelming that in any unbiased courtroom in the world it would be declared to be an historical fact.

Every shred of evidence for the resurrection of Christ is evidence for eternal life in heaven. For that same Jesus said: "I am he that liveth, and was dead; and, behold, I am alive for evermore ... Because I live ye shall live also ... I go to prepare a place for you" (Revelation 1:18; John 14:19; John 14:2, KJV).

Another evidence is that of dying. In my library there are a number of books containing within them the last words of thousands of famous people when they came to the place of death. One thing is absolutely clear—those who believed in Jesus Christ died in a way remarkably different from those who did not. An unbelieving psychiatrist heard the evidences for the resurrection of Christ presented. This man said that he had "seen enough people die to know that there is a difference between an evangelical Christian dying and anyone else."

One can see it in the writings of last words. On one page of a book on how we face death we find the words of a noted infidel, Edward Gibbon—"All is dark." Another page gives us the last words of Augustus Toplady, author of the hymn "Rock of Ages": "All is light, light, light!"[7]

Thousands and thousands of people have been granted some presentiment of that which was to come. They have seen a foretaste of the glory that was theirs; they have seen those who have died and gone before, and in those final minutes before they have left this world, heaven has opened up before them and given them a vision of the world to which they were about to go. For others, hell also has opened its mouth to swallow them. "Demons are in the room and are about to pull me down," cried the infidel Adams. The final words of the most famous of this world's skeptics and atheists are enough to make your blood run cold.

New evidence that goes even further has been given to us recently by physicians who have studied death. These psychiatrists began to encounter the phenomenon of people pronounced clinically dead who were resuscitated—at first two or three, then more and more. Between them, the physicians examined over 500 people who have died and come back.

These people have described either a place of beauty, wonder, joy, and peace, or they have described something terrible. These people have floated out of their bodies, and though out of their bodies they had bodies that were real, and though blind they could see while they were called "dead" by doctors. They tell about who came into the room, what those persons looked like, and what they did. Yet, when they were brought back, the blind could not see.

A doctor told me recently of his experience in attending a man who had been pronounced clinically dead. He succeeded in resuscitating the man, who then sued the doctor for bringing him back into this miserable existence from the glory he had experienced. One woman, describing her situation after she had suffered a respiratory arrest, said the doctors who were trying to resuscitate her were pounding on her body trying to get her back while she was over them, looking down, and saying, "Leave me alone!"[8] There was such peace, wholeness, happiness, joy, and love as they had never experienced before—an evidence which perhaps God has given in these unbelieving days to convict even the most skeptical.

My friends, I am convinced there is a life after this! Life goes on; it does not cease. The question is not whether but simply where we will spend eternity. For though there is a heaven, which the Bible abundantly makes clear, it makes it equally plain that not everybody is going there. Listen to the words of Jesus: "Enter ye in at the strait gate: for wide is the gate, and broad is the way, that leadeth to destruction, and many there be which go in thereat: Because strait is the gate, and narrow is the way, which leadeth unto life, and few there be that find it" (Matthew 7:13-14).

We will live forever, somewhere! For some it will be in bliss and felicity of heaven, where the mind of man and the heart of man never have conceived what glories God has prepared for those that love and trust Him. Others will live never-endingly in hell! Ignore it, laugh at it, repress it, suppress it, but this will happen nonetheless!

How then does one go to heaven? Thomas said, "Lord, we know not whither thou goest; and how can we know the way?" (John 14:5, KJV). So many follow in Thomas's train, not knowing the way. Jesus answered him, "I am the way, the truth, and the life: no man cometh unto the Father, but by me" (v. 6, KJV).

The way to heaven is as narrow as the Cross. Only those who are willing to humble themselves and acknowledge their sin and place their trust in the Son of God who died in their stead will ever enter the gates of heaven.

There are two personal truths I know about myself. The first is: I ought to go to hell because that is where I belong. In ten thousand times, ten thousand ways, in word and thought, omission and commission, I have transgressed the holy law of God. I stand guilty before God, condignly deserving His just displeasure. But the second truth, which I know equally, is that I am going to heaven because Jesus Christ went to hell on a cross for me. I have no other hope but Him and His free gift.

1. Leslie D. Weatherhead, *After Death* (New York: Abingdon Press, 1936), 19.

2. Thomas Curtis Clark, ed., *The Golden Book of Immortality* (New York: Association Press, 1954), 4.

3. Madison C. Peters, *After Death—What?* (New York: Christian Herald, 1908), 165.

4. Ibid.

5. Watson Boone Duncan, *Immortality and Modern Thought* (Boston: Sherman, French & Co., 1912), 33, 36.

6. Quoted in Peters, *After Death—What?* 166, 167.

7. S. B. Shaw, *How Men Face Death* (Kansas City, Mo: Beacon Hill Press, 1964), 44, 63.

8. Raymond A. Moody, Jr., *Life After Life* (Atlanta: Mockingbird Books, 1975), 37.